Stefanie Armstrong
845-553-5870

Praise for Soulmates & Strangers:

"What could be more beautiful than the story of an enduring friendship lasting close to 70 years, between two people who, when it began with the exchange of two letters, didn't even know each other? This friendship is passed on from one generation to another, from mother to daughter, and centers around two women living on opposite sides of the Atlantic Ocean. Using her compelling story-telling experience and great affection for her mother and her "French parents", Judith Umlas recounts a real adventure – nothing added, nothing embroidered. Through the writing of this book, Judy has accomplished a real, precious, and difficult piece of historical research in trying to reconstruct as much as possible about the 70 years of uninterrupted friendship. She has brought together and arranged everything that she collected in the USA and in France to tell the story of these two friends, inseparable until severe illness and death."

— **Le recteur Alain Bouvier**
Professeur associé à l'université de Sherbrooke;
Co-directeur de la collection Profession cadre Service public
(Family friend of Claudia & Mario Mariotti, friend and mentor to Judy Umlas)

"This book is a thoroughly touching, and at many times humorous, tribute to a mother, a friendship, and a time past. In the form of letters written between her mother and French pen pal, the author received the unique inheritance of insight into a period of her parent's life of which she would have otherwise been unaware. How rare it is for a grown daughter to be given a life-altering glimpse into the hopes, challenges, and thoughts on culture and current events of her mother's formative years. In turn, she passes this gift, along with an appreciation for the French language and culture, on to the reader. The thoughtful inclusion of photos, a selection of letters, the "Cast of Characters", and other supporting artwork adds a certain "je ne sais quoi" to an already artfully laid out story. Part personal memoir, part history lesson, this book is an entirely enjoyable as well as valuable exploration."

— **Anya Berg**
Adult Services Librarian, Valley Cottage Library

Praise for Soulmates & Strangers:

"I feel honored to know Judith in a whole new and deeply gratifying way, through her latest book, *Soulmates & Strangers*. As a sounding board and feedback giver to Judith as she developed and wrote ground-breaking business books, including *The Power of Acknowledgment* and *Grateful Leadership*, I thought I knew her well. However, *Soulmates & Strangers* gave me a whole new and intimate look into her life, her relationship with her mother, and other family members. The treasured letters from her mother to her French pen pal featured in the book are a priceless gift from a young girl to her future daughter and they provided Judith with an unprecedented glimpse into her mother's life, her hopes, and her dreams as a young woman. Told through the eyes of those who witnessed the challenges of the 20th century, including a World War, food shortages, and the pain of entire neighborhoods giving up their sons, the pen pal's heartfelt letters provide insight into the similarities between cultures, across time and space."

— *E. LaVerne Johnson*
Founder, President & CEO, International Institute for Learning, Inc.

Soulmates & Strangers

Best wishes,

Judith Umlas

Soulmates & Strangers

A friendship that lasted a lifetime

Judith Umlas

Soulmates & Strangers is a work of non-fiction.

Copyright © 2022 by Judith Umlas

All rights reserved.

Title: Soulmates & Strangers/Judith Umlas

ISBN: 979-8-9862848-0-4

Published in the United States by:

Handler & Wagreich Publishing, LLC

Publishing with a Purpose™

Non-Fiction, Memoir, Historical

❋

Book Design: Maria Scharf Design

Cover Design: Renee Avery-Boyd

Art Direction Collaboration: Mary Tiegreen

Edited by: DeAnna Burghart

This text is printed on acid-free paper

handlerandwagreich.com

Dedication

To the two beautiful, high-spirited, passionate young
girls who remained pen pals for close to 70 years,
Sylvia Handler Wagreich &
Claudia Raymonde Bouillard Mariotti,
I will love you both forever!

※

And to *Mario Mariotti*, my French father
(Claudia's husband) who passed away on May 10, 2021,
I love you, too!

Also by Judith Umlas

The Power of Acknowledgment

Grateful Leadership: Using the Power of Acknowledgment to Engage All Your People and Achieve Superior Results

You're Totally Awesome! The Power of Acknowledgment for Kids

Contents

Introduction	1
The Mother I Never Knew	11
A Joyous Connection	19
Judy's Visit 1965	25
Tastes, Trends, and Traditions	26
New Lives, renewed Connections	39
Embracing Joie de Vivre & the True End of the War	47
Loving and Learning	59
Creating a Home	65
New York Beginnings	73
Feathering the Nest	85
Soulmates and Strangers, bien sûr	93
A New Year, a New Life?	103
The Last Letter	109
About the Author, Judith Umlas	117
Acknowledgments	119
Cast of Characters	126
La Galerie des Personnages	127

"Before email or Facetime, when snail mail was the only way to communicate across oceans, my mother and her French pen pal created a family legacy. Their writings to one another, starting when they were teenagers and ending in their 80's, preserve a precious time in the past, while inspiring generations of the future."

Introduction

Sitting in the cramped seat of a jetliner headed to France, I desperately tried to gather the courage to read the letters that Claudia, my mother's pen pal of seventy years, had given to me five years before, when my son and I visited her and her husband in Lyon.

I've always referred to Mario and Claudia as "my French parents" whenever I spoke about them to anyone, because of the remarkable summer I spent with them when I was eighteen—a life-altering visit arranged by my mother.

I've always known that I'd been a major beneficiary of my mother's long and rich relationship with her French

pen pal. Though they never met until years after my first visit to France in 1965, I was their chosen emissary. After four years of high school French, which I adored, my mother had asked me if I wanted to visit her pen pal and her husband. She had already written to her *correspondante* (pen pal) to ask whether she and her husband could handle having an "American daughter" for a summer when they'd never had any children of their own.

For years I had heard tales of Claudia Raymonde, whom I and all of her friends knew always by her given first name, Claudia. Only my mother seemed to have the special privilege of calling her Raymonde—and later on, when she felt more comfortable, I guess, Ray. I loved hearing about how Claudia and my mother had bonded for life after one language teacher in France and another in America traded students' names and addresses. At that time, my mother was a junior in high school. From that first letter in 1936 to the last in about 2002, when my mother started her decline, their correspondence and interactions nurtured a devoted friendship

Every December, for example, for as long as I could remember, a mysterious and festive holiday package would come to our home, filled with goodies for every member of our family—fashionable clothing items like gloves, hand-knitted scarves and hats, bonbons, soaps, candles and whatever thoughtful additions Claudia could come up with for that year. My mother's shopping spree for her holiday package to Mario and Claudia began soon after summer ended. The package simply had to get there in time for Christmas! After I got married, I continued my own version of the tradition, and made sure to send special gifts to my French parents. My mother continued her part uninterrupted until she could no longer do so.

I visited Mario and Claudia in Lyon in 2005 with my teenage son, Jared. When we arrived, we were witnesses first and foremost to Claudia's ongoing obsession with "El-veese," or Elvis. I remembered it well from my visits years before, but I was surprised to see the passion persist in the heart, mind, and voice of an eighty-five-

Claudia, Judy, Mario (and Elvis) having lunch out during one of the trips to France

*The first and last of Sylvia's
letters to Claudia that
she preserved in a lace envelope*

year-old woman! An officer of "Les Amis d'Elvis," the official Elvis fan club of France, she had Elvis posters all over the walls of the tiny apartment. She sported an Elvis pocketbook and got dreamy eyed when listening to CDs of his songs, which she was quick to share with us.

But the real surprise came when she took a packet of letters in a beautiful lace envelope from a drawer and held them out to me. "They are from Sylvia," she told me. "Your mother wrote the first letter to me when she was fifteen and I was sixteen. I don't know what I've done with all the others—I'm so sad that I don't have them—but I did save these!" She beamed as she handed them to me. The yellowed pages and crumbling envelopes were carefully dated in my mother's hand from February 3, 1936, when she was fifteen, to March 26, 1947, when she was twenty-six and about six months pregnant with me, by my calculations. I was shocked and delighted, and started reading the first letter immediately. In her capable and expressive French, which I never realized she knew so well, my mother wrote to Claudia, *"I was enchanted to receive your letter. I read it almost 100 times until I knew it by heart. I am very happy to have a French friend."*

It was clear from this first paragraph that the package of letters was a treasure greater than any I could have imagined—it was a glimpse of my mother's life from her teen years up until the first years of her marriage to my father. I knew immediately that I had to have them. Uncertain that Claudia was actually giving them to me,

I asked with hope and great intention, "May I take these letters home and make copies of them? I will send them back to you as soon as I do."

"Of course!" she exclaimed.

So I took the treasures back with me to America and put them away for another time—a time that didn't come until five years later, when I was making my next trip to France. I kept them safely (and still have them) in the embroidered, lacy white envelope in which she presented them all to me.

I thought about the letters from time to time, but neither read nor copied them, nor returned them to Claudia. Finally, I confessed my tardiness during one of our telephone calls. "You must keep the letters," she replied. "They really should belong to you! What am I going to do with them?" I was thrilled and touched.

But my mother had already started her decline, and I found that I could not bear to glimpse the liveliness and spark of the young girl she had been as the lights in her eyes dimmed and her memories faded. So I waited ... until what or when, I couldn't be sure. But each time I tried to start the letters, the pain of the contrast between the young girl and my fading mother was simply too great.

My father, who had been deeply depressed over my mother's decline, died in October 2008, and my mother quickly followed in December of that year. It was a period of devastating losses for me, as I found myself

mourning three people: my father, the mother of my youth and middle age, and the mother I barely knew and who didn't know me. I spent a year in mourning, following the Jewish tradition of saying the mourner's prayer, or Kaddish, in synagogue every day, even though I was not very religious. The losses were so huge that I found I needed a spiritual community to help me carry and express my grief, and eventually to be able to move on among the living.

After one telephone call to Mario and Claudia, with whom I kept in pretty regular contact, I became very concerned. I had a distinct sense of déjà vu based on my parents' situations. Both seemed to be fading, and Mario especially seemed to be wondering if life was still worth living. His depressed state reminded me so much of my father's that it frightened me. Aging seemed to be an enormous challenge for them both.

But whenever I called and spoke to Claudia in my rusty French, we talked mainly about the glorious summer we had spent together when I was eighteen. She remembered even the tiniest details of my stay! As we laughed hysterically about some of my faux pas and other unusual occurrences of that summer, she seemed to come alive! She remembered the time I meant to say I was "full" after eating one of her carefully prepared, delicious meals and accidentally said I was pregnant instead. Even Mario laughed and cheered up as we spoke. Later he told me that my calls were better medicine for them both than any that a doctor could prescribe.

"From the glorious summer we had spent together when I was eighteen."

I decided I needed to pay them a visit. Claudia was then ninety and Mario was eighty-eight—I couldn't take the chance that my French parents would leave as suddenly as my American parents had. I couldn't risk losing the chance to say goodbye and to recount with them in wonderful and boring (to anyone else) detail the joyful and silly and challenging experiences of what I still call the best summer of my life.

I booked a flight and told them I was coming—in that order. I emailed Alain and Claudine, the son and daughter-in-law of their dear friends, to confirm that my French parents would be up for my visit. Fortunately, Alain and Claudine felt that it would be a most welcome experience.

Mario and Claudia were shocked that I would be coming just to see them. They kept asking me if I was coming on a business trip and adding on a visit, as if they must be an afterthought. When I told them that I was making the trip purely to see them, because I missed them so much, they were deeply moved and happy. Knowing how hard any change in routine had been for my parents, I told them I would stay in a nearby hotel rather than impose myself on their small space, and that I would come to see them every afternoon for a few hours for the five days I would be there. They couldn't get out and walk around very easily, so we wouldn't be able to go places. But it would be a joyful reunion anyway, of that I was sure.

By this time, I had come to a more peaceful place emotionally about my parents' passing—if not a fully accepting one. I sensed that I might now dare to read the treasured letters. So I decided to take them with me to France and read them on the long flight. About an hour into the flight, I pulled the first letter from Claudia's lovely embroidered cloth envelope and began reading it. Three hours later, while everyone else was sleeping, I shut myself in the tiny airplane bathroom and started to

sob. I continued sobbing for a long time, as I entered the life of the young girl I had never known—the spunky, outspoken American pop culture expert I had the joy of meeting for the first time—who would eventually become my dear and loving mother. What a gift I had been given! I couldn't believe what I learned about her that I had never known before!

This trip turned out to be the perfect time for me to express my heartfelt appreciation to Claudia for saving these treasures, and for giving them to me so generously. I wished again that my mother had saved her letters from Claudia. Then I realized that I inherited, and still had, many boxes of my parents' writings. Most were from their participation in a writer's group for over a decade, but I hoped then and still do now that someday I might find Claudia's early letters among them. If I do ever find these treasures, they might form a sequel to this memoir.

The Mother I Never Knew

S tarting with that first letter back on February 3, 1936, each letter was written half in French and half in English. After the first one, most of the letters included teacher-like corrections of each other's words, which they had both agreed they needed. Neither knew at the time that they would become teachers, my mother at an elementary school and Claudia at a nursery school, but the seeds of caring instruction by both were evident already. These young girls would later become two fully devoted educators, each a lifelong lover of learning and teaching.

When Sylvia, my then fifteen-year-old mother-to-be, expressed her great appreciation of the photo that Claudia had sent her and asked, *"Who is the other girl*

1449 Harrod Avenue
New York, New York
February 3, 1936.

Ma chère Raymonde,

    J'étais très enchanté de recevoir votre lettre. Je l'ai relu presque cent fois jusqu'à je l'ai su par cœur. Je suis très heureux d'avoir une amie française.

    Maintenant je vous dirai quelque chose de moi-même. J'ai quinze ans mais je suis très grande pour mon âge. J'ai des cheveux bruns, des yeux bruns, et un teint sombre.

    J'attends une école où il y a tous les deux jeunes filles et garçons. Je suis dans l'année troisième de "high school." Il me faut aller à cette école une année plus pour graduer. Ce semestre, j'étudie anglais, français, latin, histoire d'Europe et algèbre. J'aime le français plus que

The First Letter
February 3, 1936

with whom you are standing?" I had to laugh. My mother was always a matchmaker, even back then. *"The reason I ask you this is that I have a very nice girlfriend who would like to correspond with a girl in France. If you know of anyone, will you please ask her to send a letter to my friend Blossom?"* I chuckled over their attempts to create other well-suited pairs like themselves. In later letters, I read the poignant stories and repeated attempts they made to put other girls together. I learned about Sylvia and Claudia's sadness that the matches didn't seem to catch on, and how theirs was the only continuing relationship. Little did they know at the time that their intimate and news-filled correspondence would last for over seventy years!

The chronicle of my mother's family and of her young and exciting life were delivered with glorious and colorful details. I "listened" in awe about the goings and comings of my future grandmother, grandfather, aunts and uncles. I found out that my grandmother had gone to Colorado to be with my asthmatic aunt and her husband—for three months! Her other children (including my mother) were quite young at the time, so I found this a very unusual demonstration of my grandmother's commitment to her weakened daughter. I met my mother's pets: two cats, one kitten, a dog, and a goldfish that I never knew she had. She described each one in terms of size, color, and unusual markings, noting about the goldfish, *"Well, he is just like all other goldfish."*

I was on the edge of my cramped airplane seat as I read my mom's letter of March 1936, written in her carefully scripted and lovely French: *"The best way to explain to you what New York is like would be to tell you what I do each day."* How amazing to get an intimate glimpse of my mother's life at age fifteen! For me, it is almost like time travel! *"I wake up at 8:00 am,"* she reports, *"and after washing and getting dressed, I go to the dining room to have breakfast. Usually I have cereal, bread and a glass of chocolate milk. I only have coffee on Sundays. After eating, I leave for school. I arrive at 9:20 am."* What a reasonable schedule students had in those days! I also learn what my mother ate for lunch and for dinner, when she did her homework and for how long. These details are truly magical for me. How blessed I am to be able to know them. Each piece of information, mundane as it is, is precious. Red, brown, and blue were her favorite colors—did I ever know this? I think not. Why hadn't I ever asked her what her favorite colors were, I wonder, now that it is too late. But I am also enriched, even by the "too late" knowing.

At this point, Sylvia again beseeches Claudia for a favor. *"When my school friends see the lovely letters that you send to me, they all ask me to try to get French correspondantes for them, too. Could you please try to send me two more addresses of your friends who wish to correspond with someone in America, if you can?"*

Now comes the first of the instructive "correction of the mistakes" practice that, according to my mother,

was Claudia's great idea. Here's a sample of the many neatly recorded corrections, all done in beautifully straight columns.

Mistakes	Corrections
I was pleased to received it	I was pleased to receive it
Spinage	Spinach

"But," writes Sylvia, wanting to encourage her new friend, *"as you see, you've made very few mistakes in English. That is better than I have done writing French, I am sure."* The seeds of a good teacher are evident here: both constructive criticism and acknowledgment!

In the May 1936 letter, I learn what movies and shows my mother saw and read her brief reviews of each of them. There is *May Wine*, which took place in Vienna and was a real romance, she writes—*"both sad and happy."* The other movie Mom saw during the Easter holiday that year was *Chalk Dust*, the true story of two teachers in a big, modern school. She goes on to mention other films she has seen lately: *The Trail of the Lonesome Pine* with Fred MacMurray and Sylvia Sydney; *Strike Me Pink* with Eddie Cantor and Ethel Merman; *Gentle Julia* with Marsha Hunt, Tom Brown, and Jane Withers, a five-year-old girl; and *Special Investigator* with Margaret Callahan and Richard Dix. What a treasure chest of pop culture! Netflix, get ready to create a 1930s film festival just for me—I'm keeping a long list of every film Mom enjoyed. I want to share them with her, even belatedly,

and experience what she appreciated.

Then there are the books she read during a vacation: *Kitty* by Warwick Deeping, and *The Little Minister, Sentimental Tommy,* and *Tommy and Grizel* by James Barrie. It takes me a moment to realize this is J. M. Barrie, the author of *Peter Pan*, but I have never heard of these books, or of Deeping and *Kitty*. What a window into my mother's world and interests!

This letter also has the first reference to a boy she likes: *"Sol, who is eighteen!"* Wow, isn't he too old for my mom? What an interesting role reversal I'm experiencing! *"He lives far from me, but he comes to see me often and sometimes he takes me to the theater. I like him a lot!"* she writes. Nope, that was not yet my dashing dad. He must come in a later letter. I look forward to some early description of that particular *beau garçon* (handsome boy)!

One of the interesting parts of their budding relationship hits me when my mother writes, *"From your last letter, I can see that you like the theater very much. Most of the films that you have mentioned in your letter that you have seen, I have seen too."* Then she makes the gentle but slightly cutting remark, *"Most of those films played in America two or three years ago, but I will never forget some of them—especially 'Back Street,' 'Cleopatra' and 'The Little Colonel' with Shirley Temple. Isn't she the sweetest, most talented youngster on the screen?"*

Next she brings up another young talent of the time.

"Have you heard about Freddie Bartholomew? He is an English child who had never been on a stage until he came to America. He has made a great success here and is really very popular.... His newest picture out is 'Little Lord Fauntleroy.' ... I am afraid he is becoming even more popular than Shirley Temple."

Then she delivers some great news to Claudia: 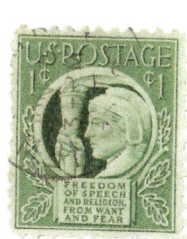 *"Because I know that you love the screen so much, I am sending you two movie magazines."* This begins their countless exchanges of cultural material—school newspapers, stamps, photos. All were valued tremendously by the recipient. Her apology for the tattered condition of the magazines is sensible (just before World War II, with all its impending sacrifices) and charming. *"When my girlfriend, Blossom, found out that I had bought two movie magazines to send to you, she made me lend them to her before I sent them to you, and when she returned them, the covers of both of them were torn off. I hope you will not be angry with me because of this. I enjoy the ones you sent me, immensely."*

And how they did enjoy trading these magazines, recipes, notecards, song lyrics, poetry and so much more, according to their letters. I am so glad that my mother referred to many of the things Claudia wrote and items she sent to her. It was clear that it was a fair exchange!

1936

Sylvia & Claudia at the ages when they were young pen pals

A Joyous Connection

I delight in my mother's charming reference to her pride in this special relationship: *"The other day, I went downtown on the subway, and I took the 'Paris Soir' with me,"* she recounts. *"As soon as I opened it up, the man and woman standing next to me looked with puzzled faces, first at me and then at the paper and the little boy seated in front of me shouted excitedly to his mother, 'Look Mother! She comes from France!' Well, you can imagine how proud I felt! I created a real sensation in that subway car."*

Another trend I see is my mother's committed efforts to have her friends, siblings, and even siblings-in-law write to Claudia in French! I am surprised, for example, to discover beautiful French thoughts and phrases written

by my aunt's accountant husband. In letters from the 1940s I see my father's efforts to write to Claudia (at my mother's request). She wanted everyone to be involved in this special relationship, and I am astounded by how well my father wrote. In those days, there was little focus on French conversation in school language programs, but the writing that all these students of the French language displayed was unbelievably good!

And now I read another letter with input in French from my mother's sister, my Aunt Adeline. *"My little one, It is I, Adeline who writes to you. I read all your letters. I like them very much. I studied French when I went to high school and college. I graduated from college in June of this year. My friend Morris* [later to be her husband] *wants to write to you the next time."* Later, Morris does try his hand. *"Hello Raymonde,"* he writes in French. *"I studied French four years ago, and I have forgotten a lot but it's interesting to try. I work in a bank. ... Thanks for reading."* Everyone wants to give this interaction a try!

The film reviews go on. My mother recounts seeing Katharine Hepburn in *Mary of Scotland* and Lionel Barrymore in *The Devil-Doll*, and *Idiot's Delight* with Alfred Lunt and Lynn Fontanne.

There are details about how my grandmother had to help my grandfather in his passementerie business (the making of buttons, bows, and other decorations for clothing). Mom writes about her mother (my grandmother to be) cooking dinner in the morning,

Judy's beloved grandmother, Sylvia's mother, Lena Handler

which my mother later heats up for her younger brother, Eddie. At eight o'clock, she says, she starts her homework and finishes between midnight and one in the morning! I never realized what a hardworking student she was. I learn that my mother goes to the tennis club on Thursdays, and the Law Club on Fridays. On Wednesdays she goes to the Akiba club—a Jewish social club—where they discuss *"the Jews in America."* Tuesdays are her favorite, though, because she stays for the French club, where *"we bring our letters from French correspondants to the club and read them."*

No wonder my mother was always pushing me to join clubs, participate in school activities, and organize gatherings and parties in our home. What a mover and shaker she was as a young girl! I would have liked to have known her then, when I was the same age as she. I wonder if we would have been friends.

Recipes are traded back and forth: *"I tried out that recipe for the cake that you sent me, as soon as I finished reading your letter,"* Sylvia writes with her usual enthusiasm. *"It really is the most delicious cake I have ever tasted. I have already baked it twice and each time I baked it, it didn't last more than two days. In my next letter I will send you a recipe book on how to make all kinds of delicious foods."* And I'm sure she sent that book to Claudia.

There are more neatly ruled "mistakes/corrections" provided:

Mistakes	Corrections
It is holidays	Holidays are here
Receipt for cake	Recipe for cake (receipt is another word meaning a bill)

There are several more. But she is certain to add encouragingly, *"I am sure that all these mistakes you made are only careless ones and not grammatical ones. Therefore, they are not bad at all. Lovingly, Sylvia."*

My mom possessed a flair for the dramatic that emerged in her letters, which I never knew existed. For example, there is this on August 6, 1936: *"My Darling Raymonde, You've been so kind and sweet to me—writing me three letters when I didn't write you one, sending me picture postal cards, and a map you must have worked terribly hard over, while I sent you nothing. I am so ashamed of myself. I am afraid to write to you. Can you ever forgive me? If you can, I will promise to be good."*

Of course, she was forgiven, after being reprimanded numerous times for her tardiness and laziness, comments from Claudia which my mother refers to with great shame. This letter also begins her commitment to visiting Claudia in France one day. *"I met a very nice boy out here"* in Far Rockaway where the family spent summers, *"whom I like very much. His name is Barney Grossman."* No, that was still not my father. *"I told him all about you, and he seemed so interested that I let him see a few of your letters. He said that when we get married, we will go to visit you for our honeymoon. Of course, he was only joking, but the first minute I get a chance, I will come to visit you."*

Ironically, Mom didn't make that visit until years after I went to spend the summer with Mario and Claudia. It was probably forty years after the first correspondence that the two devoted pen pals finally met in person, and of course it was love at first sight!

After that, it was back and forth over the years. Mario and Claudia came to stay in New York for a month in the '60s and my husband and I traveled with them while they were here, taking them camping in Washington, DC, and bringing them to visit my in-laws who vacationed each summer in Massachusetts. My in-laws then generously gave them their apartment in

Queens, NY, for the entire time they were in the US. It was a joyful and happily extended visit.

Once again I count the many blessings that emerged from the connection of these soulmates and strangers when they were teenagers. How amazing it was! I think with tremendous gratitude about my usually overprotective mother's willingness to take a big chance. As a young girl, I developed juvenile diabetes (now called type I diabetes), and yet she still allowed me to travel internationally, live with people she had never met in person, and be truly independent for the week I spent in Paris on my own following my outstanding stay in Lyon. Was it a sacrifice for her? Did she worry constantly? I'll never know, but she never interfered or intervened while I was away. Thanks for your courage, Mom! We were all the beneficiaries of it.

Claudia and Mario on one of their many excursions with Judy

*Judy's Visit
1965*

*Judy loving the Swiss lake
Mario & Claudia took her to see*

Judy meets friends of Mario and Claudia who live on a farm

Claudia and Judy sightseeing in France

Tastes, Trends, and Traditions

I love and can vividly imagine my mother's new green winter coat, with a *"flairy skirt, big balloon sleeves, and a lovely brown squirrel fur."* My mother was stunning when she was younger, and I am sure she was the epitome of fashion at that time. Here she is at about twenty years old, looking elegant in the style of the times.

In this next letter, she also hand copies three poems she loved. The first is "Little Boy Blue" by Eugene Field, which she calls *"a very sad and pretty poem, no?"*

She also shares another favorite, "Anne Rutledge" by Edgar Lee Masters, and "Smoke Rose Gold" by Carl Sandberg.

I had never read these poems, though I knew and benefited from her love of Emily Dickinson's "I taste a liquor never brewed" with the famous line that I have always loved, "Inebriate of air – am I" and a passionate poem called "Patterns" by Amy Lowell that she read to me regularly as I was growing up. I can hear her exclaim with near rage and deep sadness, "Christ! What are patterns for?" She also loved "The Congo" by Vachel Lindsay and repeatedly read it to my younger brother Carl and me. I can still hear her dramatic reading and the thumping sound she made on the table as she communicated the rhythm of the poem to us both while we sat, mesmerized.

She thus passed on to me her deep and abiding love of poetry, and now I have three more of her favorites to embrace—all written out in her hand. Added treasures.

Now she mentions another movie, *The General Died at Dawn* with Gary Cooper—who she knows is Claudia's favorite actor. *"He is superb in this movie,"* she writes, knowing full well that Claudia will have to wait two to three years to see it!

My Dearest,
    Here are three poems I love very much.

"Little Boy Blue"
Eugene Field

"The little toy dog is covered with dust,
  But sturdy and staunch he stands;
The little toy soldier is red with rust,
  And his musket moulds in his hands.
Time was when the little toy dog was new,
  And the soldier was passing fair;
And that was the time when our Little Boy Blue
  Kissed them and put them there.

II

"Now don't you go till I come," he said,
  "And don't you make any noise!"
So, toddling off to his trundle bed,
  He dreamt of the pretty toys;
And, as he was dreaming, an angel song
  Awakened our Little Boy Blue —
Oh! the years are many, the years are long,
  But the little toy friends are true!

III

Ay, faithful to Little Boy Blue they stand,
  Each in the same old place,
Awaiting the touch of a little hand,
  The smile of a little face;
And they wonder, as waiting the long years through
  In the dust of that little chair,
What has become of our Little Boy Blue,
  Since he kissed them and put them there."

IT IS A VERY SAD AND PRETTY POEM, NO?

"Anne Rutledge" (She is the wife of Abe Lincoln)
Edgar Lee Masters

"Out of me unworthy and unknown
   The vibrations of deathly music;
"With malice toward none, with charity for all."
   Out of me the forgiveness of millions toward millions,
And the beneficient face of a nation
   Shining with justice and truth.
I am Anne Rutledge who sleep beneath these weeds,
   Beloved, in life, of Abraham Lincoln,
Wedded to him, not thru Union,
   But thru separation.
Bloom forever, O Republic,
   From the dust of my bosom!"

"Smoke Rose Gold"
Carl Sandburg

"The dome of the capitol looks to the Potomac River
   Out of haze over the sunset,
   Out of smoke rose gold:
One star shines over the sunset.
Night takes the dome and the river, the
       sun and the smoke rose gold,
The haze changes from sunset to star.
The four of a thin silver struggles against the
                       dark.
A star might call: It's a long way across."

This poem describes our White House at Washington. If you liked these 3 poems, I will write you more. Lovingly, Sylvia

I now come to one of my favorite passages of any of the letters! *"I will try to speak to you a little of Hollywood, Joe Louis and of Harlem, as you are so interested in these three."* My mom speaking about these things and giving her pen pal true knowledge of the American scene? How did I miss my mother's expertise in all of these areas during my time with her? I always thought, as I was growing up, that she was a mother and therefore by definition slightly "out of it." How wrong I was! I feel both sad and excited as I begin to read the letter.

"And now for Hollywood," my mother writes. *"I shall try to give you my opinion of each of the actresses and actors that you have mentioned. First, Shirley Temple. She is a very adorable, lovely child, yet somehow or other, I never seem to enjoy her pictures. Maybe it is mean of me to say this—I don't know—but I'm afraid that if Shirley weren't such a beautiful child, her acting wouldn't be very much to rave about. What do you think?"*

Hey, wait a minute, Mom! Didn't you say you adored her in a previous letter? I suspect that over time my mother grew more comfortable with her French friend, and felt safer sharing her real opinions with her. Sadly, I feel frustrated that I can't ask her and get the true answer to my question, or even discuss their growing sense of ease with each other.

Then she moves on to Greta Garbo, *"a true actress, and a very pretty one too."* She loved her in *Anna Karenina*. *"In the end of the picture, when she dies, there isn't one person*

31

in the audience who has dry eyes. Everyone—men and women alike—is sobbing bitterly."

She admires Jean Harlow, whom she found *"adorable"* in *Suzy* and loved in *China Seas,* where she played opposite Clark Gable. Those were the days ... Joan Crawford is persona non grata for her, even though she doesn't quite know why. She hasn't seen her yet in *The Gorgeous Hussy,* where she plays opposite Robert Taylor. Katharine Hepburn is one of her favorites, especially in *Mary of Scotland.* *"In the end, when she calmly and bravely walks to her execution, once more, not one person in the audience is dry-eyed."*

"I am not very set on Marlene Dietrich." She, like Claudia, didn't like her much. However, she admits, she is *"very jealous of her"* for going around with Robert Taylor quite a bit. *"I wish I knew Bob Taylor personally!!"* my mother-to-be declares with passion.

"Have you heard of Myrna Loy?" she asks. *"She is very sweet and charming. In her latest picture, 'The Great Ziegfried,' she excellently portrays Flo Ziegfield's second wife, Billie Burke. Florenz Ziegfield is played by William Powell."* How did she know all this stuff? I never knew the actors and actresses of my day, except for a few like Doris Day and Audrey Hepburn.

Next comes Claudette Colbert, one of her favorites. *Imitation of Life* is one the most memorable movies my mother has ever seen. In it, Colbert plays a *"modern mother of a very modern daughter"* (I wonder what she means by "modern" and read on).

"Her husband has been dead for many a year, and therefore she must take the place of both mother and father to her only daughter. One evening, as she is giving a birthday party for her daughter (Rochelle Hudson), a stranger (I believe it is William Powell) comes to the party. Immediately, both mother and daughter (unknown to each other) both fall in love with this one man. He is really in love with Claudette Colbert, and only interested in Rochelle Hudson as a young girl. But when Claudette discovers that her daughter loves this man she (Claudette) is soon to marry, she sacrifices her whole life and leaves him—just so that her daughter will be happy."

Wow! (I, my mother's daughter, say to myself "Wow! What a plot!") I guess I had thought of her as a bit of a prude, but apparently she was not! She remembered the entire plot line of a film she had seen three years earlier. *"I guess that is proof enough that it was a very good picture, isn't it?"* she writes. Oh, how those young girls loved their movies and movie stars!

There aren't many good actors, according to my mom, but Gary Cooper is the best, followed by Clark Gable. *"You know Clark Gable has been in New York for 2 weeks, and he's still here. You see, his next picture will be 'Idiot's Delight,' the play that I saw last Saturday, but now they are turning it into a picture and he is to play the leading role. I am so anxious to see if he will play the part well!"* I can hear and empathize with her longing to see him. I

Page 2

My Dearest Raymonde,

I will try to speak to you a little, of Hollywood, Joe Louis, and of Harlem, as you are so interested in these three. But first, I must tell you that, if you don't mind very much, I am afraid I will not be able to send you the magazines this week. You see, this Friday, November 13, is my sister Adeline's birthday, and I am trying to save all my money to buy her a little gift, especially since she bought me a lovely gift for my birthday. But I promise, on my word of honor, tha[t] ... surely send you my se... ...azines. I [promise]...

I promise...

Page (French letter, partial)

le dix novembre, 1936.
mardi

votre lettre ce matin,
répondre. c'est
depuis je vous ai
cette fois,
é, mais depuis
ain, et il ne
... cette nuit,

Page 9

Last Saturday, Halowe'en, (do you celebrate this holiday?) I went downtown and got a coat. It is a lovely green winter coat, with a flairy skirt, big balloon sleeves, and a lovely brown squirrel fur. I will try to take a picture in it and send one to you. Last Saturday night, I went to a Halowe'en party and had a very nice time.

Next Saturday, all the girls in our club are going downtown to see a show. It is called "Idiot's Delight" Alfred Lunt stars in it. Have you heard of it? The woman star of it is Lynne Fontaine. Perhaps you have heard of her.

Today, Tuesday, nov. 3, is election

remember my movie star crushes too. But now we are on to Bob Taylor, followed by Bob Montgomery, Franchot Tone, William Powell, Dick Powell, and Gene Raymond. *"I guess that's enough for Hollywood,"* she concludes.

About Harlem, she states with an authority I never knew she possessed, *"Conditions there are mostly very poor. Things are very unsanitary. Slums prevail throughout. But traveling in a little further on, one comes to the well-known night clubs."* She goes on to describe the young women of this fascinating area *"shaking their shoulders, trucking it down (a new dance) and doing the latest—the Suzecue."* She admits she has never gone there on a Saturday night to dance and has heard that there is a lot of nude dancing. *"I've never tried it, so I don't know. Yet I imagine it would be very exciting. Perhaps one day, when I am older, I shall go to one of them, and then I shall write to you all about it. O.K.?"* I must admit I'm rather shocked by all of this—once again, it's an uncanny role reversal! How many daughters get the opportunity to see their mothers in this light, as young girls wondering about and wanting to explore the world?

Next her letter turns to boxing and the incredible popularity of Joe Louis. How the heck did my mother know anything about boxing? She never seemed to take any interest in sports at all when I was growing up. She goes on to tell how Joe Louis defeated Jack Sharkey, nearly earning the world champion title, before losing to Max Schmeling. *"He will fight Jimmy Braddock next spring, and everyone is sure Louis will win. He is a very*

serious, conscientious fellow and it seems that victory never goes to his head. After a successful bout, he is still the same simple humble Joe Louis as after an unsuccessful one! And I guess that is why his people adore him," she concludes. She's not just a fan; she's a bit of an expert, I would have to say!

Her closing to Claudia from that letter touches me. *"Well, it is pretty late now and so I guess I will leave you now, my darling. Please answer this letter and let me know what I can send you for Christmas. Please?—Your dearest Yankee, Sylvia."*

Then, in her first letter of the New Year, which is dated February 12, 1937, Mom thanks Claudia for the beauty magazine and the songs she sent her. *"I've read the magazine over and over about 30 times. I just finished playing the songs on the piano, and they are all very pretty. You know the song 'Violon Dans*

la Nuit'? Well, there is a new song out in America called 'Serenade in the Night,' and—the refrain of 'Violon Dans la Nuit' is exactly the same as our song 'Serenade in the Night.' The French goes, 'Chante, chante a moi'—You know which song I mean, don't you?"

This, I presume, was the start of the seventy-year gift exchange that I embraced, became a part of, and still share with my French father, Mario today. These exchanges continued throughout their amazing relationship, mostly through holiday gift packages filled with items native to their respective countries. What a lovely tradition that started with their early letters! And what a wonder that these young girls had such a concrete view into each other's lives and cultures—the movies, actors, actresses, music ... and boys!

In each letter, I'm being introduced to a different boy my mother dated. I think I am getting a bit of an inferiority complex. I never knew my mother was so popular, while I just had one boyfriend throughout junior high school. When he moved away in eighth grade, I didn't like or go out much with anyone until I met my husband when we were both counselors in a sleep-away camp. And that was that!

In fact, both my French and my American parents fell in love with Bob long before I did. During the summer I stayed with them, Mario and Claudia listened to my description of this talented, musical, intelligent college boy (five years older than I was) who had already asked me to marry him by the time I was seventeen. "Marry him!" said Mario and Claudia, echoing Mom and Dad. Bob certainly had a way about him, so I did marry him, and I guess they were all correct—he is the gem they all saw sparkling from the get-go, long before I did!

In her last letter of 1937, dated February 12, Mom refers to a boy named Louis K. who had asked her to go to a dance with him. *"I am very excited and happy, and wish it were next Sunday already. Louis is a very nice boy,"* she writes, *"and I like him a little."* What happened here? If she couldn't wait for their date, didn't that mean she liked him a lot? *"He has graduated from high school last year and he is now working in the daytime (his salary is $35 a week—that is a great deal of money) and he goes to college at night. He plans on being an engineer."* I am grateful that she didn't fall for Louis Kramer, or I wouldn't be sitting here writing about my precious mother and her priceless pen pal.

Wait, there's yet another boyfriend: *"Tomorrow night, I am going to the movies with Norman M., a boy I met in Rockaway. He is a very handsome boy. He will be 18 years old on March 18."* Another close call, I say thankfully to myself!

And this boy-filled, breezy letter, dated February 12, 1937, was the last correspondence my mother sent to Claudia until after the end of World War II in 1945.

New Lives, Renewed Connections

The February 1937 letter was the last Claudia and Sylvia exchanged for seven years! The next is dated New York, January 23, 1945. At first I thought that perhaps Claudia had lost the letters between those dates. Then I read the poignant, painful recounting of the war years by my mother—a true witness to what I had only read about in history books and seen in war movies. It was heartbreaking and deeply moving.

"Dearest Raymonde, I cannot tell you with what joy I received your card, written, according to its date, the 25th of September 1944. It did not arrive until yesterday—almost four months after you wrote it.... So much has happened in both of our countries—to both of us—since we last wrote."

Doing the math, I realize that in the intervening years my mother must have married the boy she never even mentioned in her other letters, although she had not only known him then but by her own admission had also loved him for some time! How odd. Could she have written about him in some of the letters that might have been misplaced? I will never know, and it will have to remain a mystery.

But on the grander scale, much more than a marriage had occurred. *"I want you to know,"* Sylvia writes, *"that I've thought of you often in the painful days that have passed—I thought of you when France fell. I thought of you often, in the days of occupation. I thought of you, again, with joy, when France was once more free."*

How amazing that all of this occurred with both my American mother and my French mother being so deeply affected. Sylvia congratulates Claudia on becoming a teacher and compliments her on her better-than-ever English. She believes that her own French, however, has suffered greatly in the interim. The last time my mother wrote to Claudia, she was still in high school. Since then, she has attended Hunter College in New York City and studied to be a teacher. When she graduated, though, she says ruefully, there were no teaching positions open, *"so I went to work as a private secretary to an attorney on Wall Street ... for three years—until December 23, 1944. Now, I have retired, and am learning how to cook and keep house. It is very enjoyable work."*

Now the kicker: *"Last February, February 27, 1944, I married someone I had loved for 9 years."* What?! Where was he when she was describing to Claudia every Tom, Dick and Harry that asked her out on a date? *"We were childhood sweethearts, but his father would not let him marry until he had finished school and his studies."* (Oh, how I remember that story.) *"He is now a dentist."* Her pride is evident as she continues, *"He is a very good husband, and I love him very much. He is 2 years older than I am, taller than I am, and—unlike me* (and very much like me, his daughter)—*he has blond hair and blue eyes and has a fair complexion. I have brown eyes, brown hair and a dark complexion* (much like my brother), *you will remember* (I assume from pictures). *We are very happy together."*

Next, she admonishes Claudia for saying she will be an old maid. Then her matchmaking instincts kick in

Fighting Soldier's Letter a Legacy of Love for Child's Mother

This is a typical attitude of an American soldier

To his only son, whom he has never seen, Sgt. Orin R. Hawkins, Jr., has written a very personal letter.

The baby, "Chip," isn't quite a year old, but someday that letter may mean more than a great deal to him. It is a legacy of love for his mother. His Daddy is with the Ninth Air Force in France—and he isn't sure he's ever going to see that son of his. He writes:

Somewhere in France,
Nov. 15, 1944.

"My Boy:

"I am writing a different kind of letter, Chip, 'cause you see there is always the possibility that I might not come back from this thing, and as much as your mother and I don't like to think about it, I have to write one about that subject so my son will have some word, something from the Dad he didn't get to see, to keep as a reminder of him.

VERY LUCKY DAY.

"And, Chip my lad, there is no better day than this one to write it. You take a look at that date up there at the top. See it—Nov. 15, 1944. Know what that date means to me? Your mommie and I were married two years ago today. Two years ago at three in the afternoon I got myself the most wonderful bride anyone could ever have—the lady who gave or read this letter to you—your mommie.

"I was very, very lucky that day, and because I was, you are lucky, too—'cause you have her for your mommie. I want you to know how lucky you are and I want you to know that she has always been everything to me.

"Tho I have never seen you, nor you me, always remember your dad loved you as if he had been there all along with you. Your mom has tried, I know, to make you conscious of your dad, and I hope she has succeeded so that if I don't ever get to see you, you'll listen to a few words from 'your old man.'

"I want you to know, son, that the most important thing is your mother. Never let that thought escape you for a moment. You have been told how much I love her and how much she means to me. I want you to carry on that love for me, and I know you will—after all she has done for you. A grander person never lived and a grander mom you could never have.

"She will have brought you up the right way, so just continue on with what she has taught you and you will never go wrong. And, above all, watch out for and take care of—all the days of your life—that lady whom I love and have loved so much.

"If I don't get back, that's a job YOU have GOT to do—that is your daddy's last and main wish. You see that she never wants for anything. She deserves nothing but the best and hasn't had much success in getting it since she has been married to me, due to the war. But you are her dearest possession.

"Your dad and a lot of other dads are over here, or in the jungles of the South Pacific, trying to put an end to war for all time. We thought our dads had done that, but they didn't know the nature of these people we are up against.

HOPE TO END WARS.

"We hope we do end it for all time, and hope we don't make the same mistake they did. I want my son to be proud of me, to be able to stand up with the rest of his playmates and be able to say his dad did his bit.

"But the most important thing is your mom. Be sure she always remains the light of your life, as she has been mine. I know you don't need any advice on that score—you've been with her and know what she is like. When Nov. 15th rolls around each year, see that she is supplied with a bunch of roses in memory of your dad.

"And just in case your dad doesn't get back, think of him once in a while, will you, Chip, for he has thought the world of you.

"Your Dad."

Baby Orin R. Hawkins, III, was born Feb. 23, 1944. His dad, the sergeant, was a Long Island boy. His parents, Mr. and Mrs. Orin Hawkins, lives at 310 Roselle ave., Cedarhurst. His wife, Barbara, now is with her parents, Mr. and Mrs. William F. Killip, of 183 Sedgewick ave., Yonkers.

Sgt. Hawkins attended Washington and Lee University and took an M. A. at Allegheny College.

and she offers to find an American for her, *"since the young men of Lyon must be scarce."* How heartbreaking a situation that was, given all the losses of young men in the war. Now she remembers a cousin of hers from New Jersey who was stationed in France for a while. *"I shall write and tell him of you, so that if he ever gets a furlough, perhaps he can come to see you. He is a very fine boy ..."*

But the most powerful part of this first letter in seven years is about the world situation. *"We have grown up into a world that is filled with pain and bloodshed. There is much sadness in America, for we do not like to wage war. The young boys have grown from careless youths to stern men, overnight."* I suck in my breath as I read this—it is so movingly and eloquently expressed. *"We each try to do our bit to hasten the end of the war,"* she continues. *"We are all in a hurry to return, once more to the peaceful days we have known."* She wants Claudia to understand that she does not want to sound philosophical, but that this is her way of telling her that *"our hearts, here in America, are not light, as they were when I wrote to you 7 years ago. We have all felt the reality of the war!"*

In true Sylvia style, she now tells Claudia that her husband sends his fondest regards. *"Perhaps he will write a few words in my next letter to you. He, like me, was very happy to see your postal card."* And then she proudly proclaims her new married name.

Included with the letter is a yellowed but still very readable newspaper clipping. It's a letter from a fighting soldier who has never seen his infant son and is writing from the jungles of the Pacific while trying to *"put an end to war for all time."* If he does not return, he tells his son to make sure that his mom remains *"the light of your life, as she has been mine."* It is a moving account, and my mother writes, *"This is a typical attitude of an American soldier."*

Nearly four months later, the next letter arrives, full of exciting news about Claudia's impending marriage—to an American boy! My mother is beside herself with joy and looks forward with great enthusiasm to her dear friend's arrival in her country. *"I only hope you will both be married soon,"* she writes, *"and will spend a long and happy life here in America, with your mother by your side.... I want to be at hand when you come to our shores."*

This is news to me! My French father Mario is not American but rather of Italian origin. What is happening here? This is like a soap opera—I can't wait until the next "episode." I am wondering why Claudia never told me about her American boyfriend. We exchanged some very personal information when I spent the summer there. I will have to explore this when I get to France, for sure!

What follows next is truly adorable. Mom cannot resist getting everyone in the family involved in this enduring and gratifying relationship. So, she writes of my beloved grandmother-to-be:

> *Mother tells me to write and tell you that she is attending evening school, to become better acquainted with reading and writing the English language. You see, she was born in Lithuania and came to the United States when she was about 20 years old. She married my father soon after, and was busy, in later years, raising her four children. So, she had little time to take care of learning to read and write the English language. Now, however, since her children are grown up, she has more time to think of herself, so she has been attending evening school. Well, she told me she would be glad to have you come along, if you thought you needed some additional schooling.*

I have always adored my grandmother and thought of her as a source of pure, unconditional love and perfection. And yet I had no idea that she went to night school! I continue to be amazed by all these revelations.

Then Claudia must have expressed some concern about meeting my mother at last. *"I do not think you will be bashful when we meet, for the first time,"* she reassures her. *"It will be like meeting an old friend, and I am sure we will be good friends from then on. We will have much to say to each other, I am sure."* Yes, soulmates and strangers ... how remarkable!

Sylvia speaks with gladness about the end of the war in Europe that year, but says, *"Here, we still have another war to fight with the* [expletive] *Japanese. It is really heartbreaking. But now that the Nazis' power has been broken, we can concentrate all our fighting power against the Japanese. I hope this war will soon be over, too, and that the world may once more settle down to the ways of peace and happiness."* Amen, Mom. May your wish come to pass in these challenging times, too.

Embracing Joie de Vivre & the True End of the War!

It is summer now, and Mom and (yes!) Dad have been away at a hotel for a two-week summer vacation! She returns to find two letters from Claudia and is so happy to hear from her—especially after the long separation they endured during the war. Sylvia tells her in vivid detail about the other young couples at the hotel, many of them from the Bronx, too. *"We played and sang and danced together on this long-awaited vacation"*—their first, it seems since Paul, my father, has opened his dental office. *"In the daytime, we all played ball together—we played tennis, basketball, baseball, volley ball [my mother?] and in the evening, we danced to an orchestra, and saw shows, right at the hotel."*

She tells a curious story about a young couple on their honeymoon who *"did not tell us this until they were ready to go home to the Bronx, for they were afraid the boys would tease them, as most Americans tease and laugh at newly married couples. Do they do that in France, Ray dear?"* Sylvia wanted to know. *"We could not tease this new couple, for at first they told us they had been married for 3 years, though actually, they'd been married for only 3 days."* How peculiar!

Then she apologizes for writing for three pages about the vacation, without even mentioning the big news—the end of war with Japan! *"We are all so very happy about it—you must have read in your newspapers how we feel about it. It feels too good to be true. We waited so long for the war to end. It is almost four years that we were at war, and we were indeed tired of the fighting and killing of our youth,"* she writes plaintively. *"We, too, suffered from food shortages and black market, even as you, in France do. Food is still not plentiful in America, and there is always a shortage of something—eggs, butter, bread, milk, and especially, of meat. Right now, it is difficult to get soap, for people, fearing a shortage, began to buy up and horde the soap, and now there is none to be had. Sugar, too, is not yet plentiful, although there is more now than there has been for the last few years."* I remember how I had to study about this in school and how it never seemed real to me—now I have it directly from someone experiencing these hardships. I had never heard these details from her before. What a waste, I feel with some guilt and much sadness.

The next passage surprises me: *"So, our war with Japan has ended, we hope, just as it finally ended with Germany. What everyone wants most is peace, once more, and normal peacetime living. (But) our boys are still overseas—in Europe and the Pacific, and I suppose it will be many years before they all return home."* What a shame! I try to remember any of the details of the dry history textbooks I was forced to read and memorize. *"War plants (factories making instruments of war) have begun to close down and peacetime factories,*

making radios, automobiles, washing machines, furniture, etc., have begun to open, which is a good sign of peace."

Her own small street is celebrating the victory, for *"even on this small street, many mothers' sons have fought and died—some are missing—some are wounded. Everyone who lives here has given $1.00 for a party, to be held in the street."* What a joyful and thrilling celebration that must have been, and using their hard-earned dollars represented a real commitment to expressing their release, relief, and fun for the first time in years.

Now she comes back to the world of cinema. It has been many years since their heated discussions about the best and the worst of the film and theater scenes. *"I, too, used to be very fond of Gary Cooper, but in the last presidential election, when Franklin Roosevelt ran against Thomas Dewey, Gary Cooper spoke unkindly of Franklin Roosevelt and since then, I have not been too fond of Gary Cooper. Since then, too, we have lost our beloved President Roosevelt, and we still mourn his untimely passing."* I know that it wasn't likely that I would have learned of this historical detail from a textbook and feel honored to receive it directly from my mother.

She says her favorite actor is now Clark Gable, who has been *"very brave in this World War II and has not made a film for many years. He suffered keen personal loss, too, when his wife, Carole Lombard, died in an airplane crash on her trip to sell war bonds for this country."* That detail sounds familiar, but hearing about it from a witness of the times is a privilege. She also commends Bette Davis for her great acting, but thinks she is not very pretty. Oh well—having both acting talent and beauty is not easy!

Now comes sad news about Claudia. *"As for your Louis, I was very unhappy to learn in your first letter, that you no longer heard from him. I was hoping you would marry him and I hope all will be well again between you."* She notes their differences, which Claudia must have described to her, and advises her friend to *"make sure you are in love with Louis, if you still want to marry him, for without love, marriage can be very sad. If you are in love with each other, you will overcome all else."* And now, she says, she has to close the nine-page letter, as she must start to cook supper. *"I am not a very good cook, but my husband is kind, and says everything I cook is good, even though it may not be good.... Sometimes I burn things, too, but he always eats it, anyhow. He is a dear!"* That's my dad, who always loved to eat!

The next letter is dated October 6, 1945. Just seeing the year written down projects me, like an enthusiastic time traveler, into an era I've never felt overly interested in. I feel a twinge of guilt over this disinterest, but drink in Mom's every word about this time and its events—and how they relate to her, to her *correspondante*, and to the world.

It is Saturday night, *"the night when most people go out— to the movies, to a dance or to a nightclub (café). However, Paul and I are very tired tonight, so, instead of going out,*

we are spending a quiet evening at home, each writing letters to our friends." How homey and cozy that sounds. I am touched by the simplicity of their being together—no computers, no emails, no extra work to complete on the weekend, not even a mention of television, which I think came much later. How romantic!

Mom has been trying to find the song sheet for "Stardust," which Claudia had requested of her. I remember Mom loving that song, too. *"I inquired after it at several stores, but no one seems to have it, since it is a very old song."* Older than 1945? Is that possible? *"I, too, am very fond of it, as is my eldest sister, Esther. When she was much younger (she is now 30), one of her then boyfriends gave her the record of the song 'Stardust,' and Esther played it very often. As a result, I got to know, and like, the song very much. I shall continue to look for the song in the stores and hope I shall find it; if I do, I shall send it to you immediately."*

I begin to hatch an idea—one that I know will bring great joy to my French parents. Maybe I can find a music store and get a CD of "Stardust" for Claudia. I know she has a CD player, as she filled our ears with Elvis last visit. What fun that would be, to play a song that I would bet she has not heard in over 50 years! Maybe she and Mario will even dance to it!

In fact, when I presented the gift to them a few days later, they were both very touched and did dance to the still familiar strains of the song. I was deeply moved by

Mario and Claudia finishing a dance to "Stardust" with a kiss! (Judy is very happy to see this!)

this and so glad that I had learned about Claudia's love of the song, along with that of her pen pal Sylvia.

I adore Mom's description of her quest for an office for my dad. This is so exciting! I heard very little about this process from either of my parents. *"Until now, he has been working with another dentist,"* she writes with obvious pride, *"but he now wishes to open his own office."* Then she describes the great difficulty in finding one, *"because there is a great housing shortage in our country."* She bemoans the fact that *"one cannot find an apartment. I go downtown each day, to look for an office. I hope I will have luck soon and will find one. My husband is very anxious to begin his own practice and I am eager to be his assistant. I shall work with him, at first, at any rate, and, if I enjoy it, I shall make a career of being a dental assistant to my husband."*

I now recall seeing a black and white photo of Mom in a white uniform assisting my father in an office. There are some prank photos, too, of Dad sporting a Groucho Marx moustache while working on a patient. They seemed to be so in love and look as if they were having such a good time. That was not always the case when I was growing up, and I relish this "honeymoon" tale. *"He is so sweet and kind, I shall enjoy working with him, I am sure."* Hmmmm ... Then why did you become a teacher, Mom? Maybe once my brother and I were born it made more sense logistically, but it does make me wonder how the dentist and dental assistant roles worked out—or didn't! I am also very eager to learn the details of finding that apartment, which my brother and I both vividly remember—a living space combined with a dental office, with one shared bathroom.

My brother and I still chuckle over one of the more comical moments in that combined living and working space. Walking past a waiting room full of patients, my three-year-old brother went to the shared bathroom and, after spending some time in it, yelled out at the

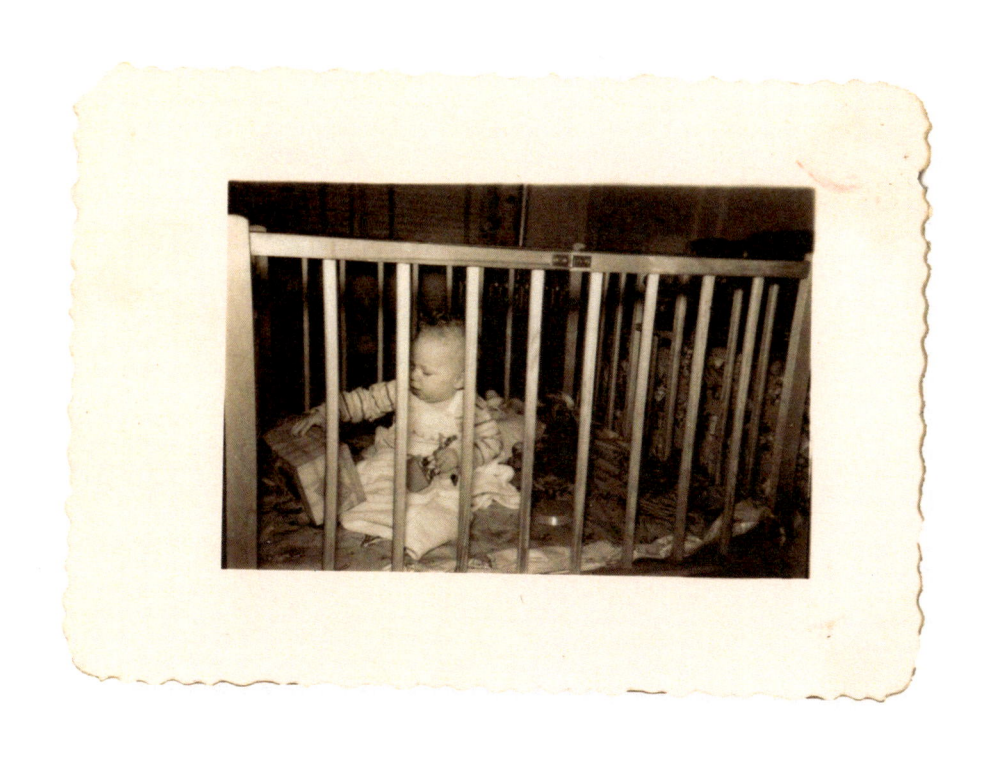

Infant Judy in the
Bronx apartment
1947

top of his little lungs, "Mommy, come and wipe my tushy!" I have a vague sense of the laughter of the patients and the less than pleased response of Daddy, the dentist. We did move to a house about two years later. Maybe that was one of the reasons why!

But before I can find out more about our childhood home, I get to see a bit more of the post-war world through my mother's eyes. *"Ray dear, you ask if I am a Jitterbug."* Now what does that mean, I wonder? I thought one *did* the jitterbug, not that one *was* one. I think a little research is in order here, so I can be sure I know what I am reading about. I discovered that the term jitterbug came from slang used to describe alcoholics who suffered from the "jitters" and later became associated with swing dancers who danced without even knowing the dance or showing any control or knowledge of the dance they were doing. They just kind of cut loose and moved in whatever ways they felt like.

Mom responds to Claudia's question, *"No, I am not. It*

is for younger people, not for me (I was just 24 years old)." Imagine, she sees herself as older and yes, her birthday was September 26, so the date had just passed. *"Boys and girls of 13 to about 17, are usually jitterbugs, and not all, of course, are."*

She closes her letter with her assessment of the political scene. *"I read of affairs in France with much interest. The other day, I read in the newspaper that politics are becoming more steady and settled in France. I hope the unrest is at an end, and that the world will settle down, once more, to peacetime living."* I never knew my mother as a keen political observer—I don't remember ever discussing world politics at our dinner table. At election times, there would be some brief discussion of the candidates and the issues, but my parents always, as far as I knew, simply voted as Democrats—straight down the ballot.

But in this letter to her French friend she observes with interest. *"Here in America, we are having our period of unrest. There are many labor strikes, where workers ask for more wages and less hours, but each strike is settled peaceably. There are many problems to face in a peace time world, but we must deal patiently with each one. It is good to have peace once more. It is good, too, to see the boys return home, though there will be many who will never come home. Yes, war is terrible!"* I can almost hear her exclaiming "Christ, what are patterns for?" Now I understand better her passion and empathy with Lowell's tragic poem.

❝ *I never felt stupid or sensed any impatience on their part.* ❞

Claudia and Mario giving Judy their intense listening and helpful communication.

Loving and Learning

Mom implores Claudia to write a little in French in the next letter (had she been writing strictly in English?) *"I want to see if I still remember how to read French. I have not read it since my college days, four or five years ago."* I understand—I always feel I have lost what I learned until I find myself speaking with Claudia. She speaks a perfect, incredibly understandable French and always seems to know what I am trying to get across, even if I am struggling. Then she gently says what I meant or wanted to say in her perfect, professorial French and I "record" it in my mind for future use. That is how I spent the summer with them all those years ago. I never felt stupid or sensed any impatience on their part. What generous, wonderful, lovable people I have had the grace and good fortune to know and love. All because of my mother. Thank you, Mom, I say again and again, for this magical gift that has enriched me all these years.

As I write this, I wonder how much longer I can possibly have my French mother. She will soon be ninety-one, and I can sense her increasing frailty. These are painful thoughts, especially with her being so far from me. Mario, too, is fading, but he fades with strength, drama about how hopeless it all is, and how I am such good medicine for them. But recently, he has not wanted to put Claudia on the phone with me. She is always sleeping. "Well, wake her up," I say in my fractured French, and sometimes he does and we have a wonderful conversation. And sometimes he doesn't ... I am dreading the news I know will be coming one day and feel helpless to deal with it. So, for now, I continue reading. I must preserve this beautiful woman who saw the magnificence of my mother and loved and treasured their friendship all these many years. This helps, and lets me preserve the joy, the energy, the connection of these two young women, these pure, energetic sparks! Once again I think how blessed I am to have these letters.

The next one is dated December 13, 1945. I think about how fortunate I am to have the exact date of each letter. I can see sequences, consequences, follow ups, promises made, promises broken. And never is the connection destroyed. Not even now, with my mother gone and Claudia possibly going, is that connection damaged or broken. I carry it forth within me, within my experiences, in these precious letters, in my stories I tell anyone who will listen: "It was the best summer of my life," I always say.

For many years I felt slightly guilty for saying that when I have had so many wonderful experiences with my husband—Morocco, Iceland, Sweden, Norway, camping on an island in the middle of Lake George. So I made myself say, "It was one of the best summers of my life." Then, this summer, when I visited my French parents and carried the precious letters back with me,

Judy's husband, Bob, with Claudia on one of the couple's many trips to France

I struck the "one of" from my descriptions and gave it its due. It *was* the best. Being with instant family I had never met before, learning the language, laughing in French, singing in French, visiting people and places I had never known or imagined before ... it was *formidable* (wonderful, amazing). It was without a doubt the best summer of my life, and now I can say I'm proud, rather than ashamed, of that.

Reading these letters, I am grateful for the date, written clearly in my mother's hand. In essays she wrote years later as part of a writer's group she organized, she would often write the month, and sometimes the date, but almost never the year. I have wondered so many times as I read and reread those essays what was happening in our family and in my life when she wrote these revealing and wondrous pieces. I can only guess. But in these treasured letters, all is clear and historically factual.

In this letter, she thanks Claudia for writing partly in French. *"I was thrilled that I am still about able to read and understand the French part of your letter. I was afraid I had forgotten how to read French. I shall be very happy if you will continue to write part of your letters in French, as you did this time. Perhaps, in that way, I shall recall all the French I used to know."* I empathize with my mother. Each time I pick up the phone to call Mario and Claudia I experience palpitations, fearing that I will be unable to communicate with the people I love so dearly. Such a natural ability—to speak a common language—is completely dependent on my memory and comfort level. Of course, when I am surrounded by the language, for example when I visit France, it returns to me very quickly. I am always amazed at how the words seem to fly into my brain. "Where did that word come from?" I wonder, and feel a profound gratitude that I have so much tucked away in my mind that I'm not even aware of, that returns when I am surrounded by the beautiful sound of the language.

Mario & Claudia at a Party

80 Strong Street
Bronx, NY
Sylvia & Paul's
first apartment & dental office

Creating a Home

"*I am happy to read that you attend the American canteen,*" Mom writes. "*Before I married, I used to be a hostess in a canteen in New York, and I found it very interesting. I met soldiers and sailors from Australia, Canada, France, Britain, and from every state in the United States. It's a thrilling experience, and I know you must enjoy your work at the canteen.*"

Really?! I never knew about this, and get such a kick out of knowing now. Did we ever talk about those experiences, Mom? I don't remember them at all, but maybe I didn't give you the attention you deserved when you shared stories of your youth with me. I was much more interested in my own fascinating stories, and you seemed to be as well—always curious, always questioning, always secretly and not so secretly arranging parties with opportunities for me to dance cheek-to-cheek with my seventh-grade sweetheart!

Always looking for connections to Claudia and to her world, she writes, *"Do you ever meet any American boys from New York?"* What a thrill that would have been for her, and I'm sure the questions about where they lived, who their friends were, what they did for entertainment, would have come flying if there had been any boys from New York.

I can almost hear her sadness and frustration as she continues, *"We know many boys who are still overseas—some in France, some in Germany, some in Italy. Most of them, especially the married boys, are very eager to return to their own countries, and to take up living normal lives, as they did before the war began."*

But now there is exciting personal news to share: *"We have found an apartment—which is a very difficult thing to do these days. We are very happy about it, and can hardly wait 'til we move in."* At last I get the firsthand description of the apartment that my brother Carl and I have tried to visualize and recreate from our memories for so many years. *"It is a 5-room apartment, and we shall use 3 rooms for ourselves (kitchen, living room and bedroom) and*

2 rooms for our dentist's office (waiting room and operating room)." She goes on about all the repair work that must be done before they can move in: *"plumbing, carpentry, electrician and painter must each do his job."* It will take another three or four months for the apartment to be ready. *"You know,"* she says plaintively, *"we are married almost 2 years, and we have been living with my parents and brother, in their house, all this time. Now, at last, we will have a home of our own."* I can feel her pride and her optimism.

Then I learn about how difficult it is to buy furniture. *"We must wait 2, 3 or even 4 months before we can get certain pieces."* And I thought 2, 3 or 4 *weeks* was too long for items my husband and I have ordered! *"Still,"* she concludes, *"it is all a thrilling experience. I shall not only keep house for my husband, but I shall also act as his nurse, in his dentist's office. I think I shall enjoy the work very much."*

She speaks next of her sister Esther and her husband Dan, plus their daughter Joanie, age three, who have been living with Mom, Dad, my grandparents and my uncle, since my aunt cannot find an apartment of her own. *"It is very nice to have my sister with us again, even though her little daughter sees to it that the house is never quiet … she is very clever, and has a good, logical mind. It is very interesting to hold a conversation with her. The other day,"* Mom reported, *"I spoke to her of God, to see what her little mind knew of the Supreme Being. She told me that God was a doctor, who cured sick people."*

*Sylvia's sister Esther
& her baby, Joan*

My cousin Joan withdrew from our entire extended family when she was in her twenties and has had little or no contact with any of us since. I have always wondered why, and I appreciate this glimpse of my older cousin at this young age. I still have fond feelings and sadness at losing connection with her.

Mom then writes about her sister Adeline's daughter, Joyce, who was four at the time. *"She is another clever little girl,"* Mom reports, *"but very different from Joanie.*

Sylvia's sister Adeline & her daughter, Joyce

My sisters want me to hurry up and have a little one of my own, but I tell them they'll have to wait awhile." This comment makes me think of all the pressure I got from my mother—and many others—to have a child soon after I got married. My husband and I had waited sixteen years before having our first child, until we were good and ready. By then, my parents had given up on the idea of ever getting a grandchild from me. Going by the date of my mother's letter, though, we are less than a

" I think back to Claudia's mother. She was lovely, patient, and kind... "

Claudia and her mother, Jeanne Seguin

year away from my own conception!

She laments her inability to buy holiday gifts this year, *"for my Paul is not working, and we must save all our money for our new home and office. I hope that next year, at this time, we will have lots of money, and will be able to buy gifts for all."* It is so interesting to me to see my parents living in the same state as my own daughter and her new husband. They too have had to watch every penny, as my son-in-law was not yet working—having just finished school and going on to a program to become a nurse. They are expecting, and our daughter just finished telling me that this year they were not able to afford any holiday gifts. I never thought of my well-established parents as once facing similar challenges.

She wraps up this letter by talking about New Year's Eve and what people do in New York to celebrate. *"We go to Manhattan (Broadway) where it is so crowded one cannot walk, or we go to a friend's house and dance and sing and drink liquor although Paul and I do not like whiskey, or we go to a movie with a few friends. It is a lot of fun."* So hard to imagine my parents drinking and dancing. And then the inevitable and charming question, *"Do you do these things in France, Ray dear?"*

The closing paragraph gives Claudia the new address, to use if she thinks her next letter will come after December 31st. She ends with her usual, *"My love to you and your Mother, from my husband and me."*

I think back to Claudia's mother. She was lovely,

patient, and kind, and the only person who picked up on a temporary and happily short-lived bout of homesickness I had when I was there. *"Tu as le cafard,"* she said to me one day, with compassion and understanding. I looked up the word in the dictionary and realized it translated literally as "to have the cockroach," but colloquially meant "down in the dumps." I had to agree. And it made me feel so much better to share this with someone who wouldn't possibly be offended by it. I can't wait to read the next letter from Mom, written in the place where my childhood memories start!

New York Beginnings

January 16, 1946

This letter is on letterhead—clear and bold and beautiful! I feel proud when I read it. I can feel both of my parents' pride at having and using it as well.

Amazingly, I realize that the phone number is one I could have accessed from my memory banks and spouted forth if asked. It is so familiar. How many other details are stored away without my awareness?

Mom writes about having received <u>four</u> letters from Claudia, and how happy this made her. *"I am very happy whenever a letter comes from you, and Paul and I always enjoy reading them so much. I hope you don't mind when*

DR. PAUL WAGREICH
80 STRONG STREET
BRONX 63, N.Y.

KINGSBRIDGE 3-5023

January 16, 1946

My dear Raymonde;

I was very, very happy to receive four letters from you. It is very sweet of you to think of us so often. I am very happy whenever a letter comes from you, and Paul and I always enjoy reading them so much. I hope you don't mind when Paul reads your letters. He enjoys them as much as I do, and is always wanting to know about you — how you are, and what you are doing, just as I am interested.

Joe Shine seems to be a very nice young man, although he weighs a lot, and must be either very strong and big, or very fat. Maybe someday I will see him, when he returns to the United States. It is very kind of you to tell him to come to my Paul when he (Joe)

Paul reads your letters. He enjoys them as much as I do and is always wanting to know about you—how you are, and what you are doing, just as I am interested."

How did Claudia really feel about Mom sharing her letters with my father? Did she consider it an invasion of privacy, no matter how minor? Did she feel she had to watch her words because Paul would be reading them as well as Sylvia, and her sister and her brother-in-law and all her friends who spoke French? Or was she exceedingly proud that she had American fans all over who wanted to read her words, hear her stories, share her cares and her joys?

Next, Mom refers to a new character in this unfolding saga, a friend Claudia must have mentioned in her letter: Joe Shine. *"Joe Shine seems to be a very nice young man, although he weighs a lot, and must be either very strong and big, or very fat."* Don't you just love her honesty? I had to giggle when I heard that one! *"Maybe someday I will see him, when he returns to the United States. It is very kind of you to tell him to come to my Paul when he has a toothache. We are opening a new office and can use many patients."* It continues to amaze me how these young women—thousands of miles apart, never having met one another in person, enter each other's lives and try to help, matchmaking and sharing physical aspects from each of their lives with the other. How intimate, and best-friends-forever-ish!

Mom goes on to describe the new apartment. *"It is a*

7-room apartment, as I think I described to you. This is how it goes" and she draws the layout.

as a toothache. We are opening a new office, and can use many patients.

I have moved into my new apartment, as you must know. We moved here two weeks ago, and find it very wonderful. It is a 7-room apartment, as I think I described to you. This is how it goes:

I know it must sound like a great many rooms. As a matter of fact it is. I found that out today, when I tried to clean the apartment. There are so many floors to wash, and so much furniture to dust. We don't have all our furniture yet, since it is so hard to get. It comes in slowly. Yesterday, we got our bed, which is French Provincial in style. It is very simple, yet lovely. Do you know how it looks? Perhaps, some day you will come to America, and you will

Then in her humble way, and almost apologizing for the abundance, Sylvia says, *"I know it must sound like a great many rooms. As a matter of fact, it is. I found that out today, when I tried to clean the apartment. There are so many floors to wash, and so much furniture to dust. We don't have all our furniture yet, since it is so hard to get. It comes in slowly. Yesterday, we got our bed, which is French Provincial in style. It is very simple, yet lovely. Do you know how it looks?"* And then she says what she seems to say at least once in every letter, in a variety of ways and in a variety of interesting pleas: *"Perhaps, some day you will come to America, and you will see my home. I am very happy with it, and I think you would like it, too."* I think once again how ironic it is that I had the honor of meeting Claudia before my mother did, and what a gift my mother gave me by appointing me as her personal emissary! I also feel a twinge of guilt, but know that everything happened in due time and right on schedule.

Their relationship had so many dimensions that meeting in person was more like icing on the cake than a necessity. That they were virtual strangers didn't prevent them from being soulmates. So it doesn't totally surprise me that even though my parents regularly took us traveling when we were children, we never went to Lyon. We always went someplace much closer and less expensive. If my mother had insisted, they would have gone. Yet it all would happen in due time. Once it began, the trips back and forth by all, starting just a few years after my summer with my newly acquired French parents, were a delight for each of us.

For now, there are more immediate concerns, and I love the pride Mom expresses. *"My Paul is busy now."* (I also love the possessiveness—I think that would have receded or disappeared by the time I would have been aware of it, but I still find it so cute!) *"He has his first patient in the chair, and I am very excited. I would like to help him, but I am afraid I would get in his way."* She goes on to recount how the first patient lived upstairs and didn't even know them but came anyway. She writes of the many newly married couples living there along with them.

That first patient, I'm told, brought my green-thumbed father a congratulatory house plant, a dieffenbachia. He nurtured and cared for it for the rest of his life, taking cuttings and creating many new plants. From that original plant, just about every member of our extended family took cuttings; my son Jared has one that has grown to be nearly six feet tall! My brother Carl is our dieffenbachia "dealer" and makes cuttings for any family member who wants one. Now I know how we came by that first plant—it was from their first patient.

Next comes a birthday wish to Claudia, combined with some sadness. *"I want to send my best wishes to you on your recent birthday. I hope you had a very happy day, and that the year that lies ahead will be a happier one than the last few years have been. I know there is much hardship for you in France, and I am unhappy when I think of all the*

Jared's Dieffenbachia

hardships you must undergo. It can't be for always, they say, and so, I hope you will take courage from the thought that 'this, too, shall soon pass' (I quote from the Bible)."

I feel the slight shock of profound connection with these words, as though I am hearing them from their source for the first time. For years, it has been very common for me to say to a friend or business associate having difficulties, "As my mother would say, 'this, too, shall pass.'" I have said that countless times, and never knew that, at least according to my mother, these words came from the Bible. The phrase, it turns out, is credited both to Persian Sufi poets and to Solomon in Jewish folklore. Well, I have found *my* source, and that is all that counts.

She is shocked by how little a teacher in France is paid. *"Here,"* she says, *"teachers are not rich, but they make at least $40 a WEEK, and often, more."* Yes, those were big dollars, then.

And then comes yet another plea for a visit from Claudia: *"Perhaps, someday you will come to America, and will teach French in America. Won't you try to come!? Perhaps Sgt. Joe Shine will miss you when he comes to America and will send for you. I hope he will. Do you like him enough to marry him?"* I don't know

Claudia's response at the time, but I do know that she never did marry Sgt. Joe Shine. What an interesting epic, though, with Claudia and her attraction to American boys! I wish I had known that when I stayed with her. I did mention one of the American soldiers when I was with her a few years back, and she coyly claimed not to remember him or any other. I don't quite believe it, though; she remembered so many other details from the past!

The money problems continue. *"We spent a quiet New Year's Eve. We have very little money now, for we have spent all our money to furnish our home and office, so we could not go where it cost much money."* But that didn't stop them from having fun by going to the movies with a bunch of friends, and then to my Aunt Adeline's house after, where they stayed until three o'clock in the morning. Wow! I never knew Mom to stay up *until* midnight on New Year's Eve, let alone that far beyond it. *"It was a very pleasant evening, and it cost us nothing. My brother-in-law paid for our movies. He is a very fine fellow, an accountant by profession. I am very fond of him."*

That was a new take on my uncle. By the time he divorced my Aunt Adeline and married the woman he had apparently been keeping house with for most of the time he was married to my aunt, our whole family had grown to dislike him. I wish the fondness my mom felt for him could have been sustained by appropriate actions on his part. It was almost an unspoken agreement that we had to shun my uncle, as he was hurting my aunt so much. The letters were making him into something more than a cardboard bad guy.

After describing their pleasant New Year celebration, Mom recounts all the visitors who come to their new home. Her whole family had been there the day before, and she was so happy to have them. Today, she is expecting Dad's oldest brother, his wife, and their two children. She is worried about the time it took for people to find out how good a dentist her husband is—*"My Paul is a very good dentist!"* I do love that possessiveness! I wish I could have seen that while I was growing up, when there was a fair amount of discord, though still great love, between them.

She bemoans the fact that the apartment takes so much time from her day that she doesn't have time to read a newspaper, but, she says, *"I know that wartime prosperity has gone, and that our country, as well as yours, is faced by very serious problems, foremost amongst which is the strife between labor and capital—the worker and the boss. The country is tied up with strikes—telephone, meat, steel, glass, almost every industry has its strikes. I pray the trouble will soon be over, but it will not be solved so easily. We must be patient."*

I am once again so surprised to hear my mother on a political platform, speaking out against such conditions. I had never known her to voice her opinions in this manner, to take a stand, and it is like hearing someone I never knew. I remember a time when my social studies teacher called Mom in for a parent-teacher conference to make her aware of my total lack of knowledge of current events. Give me creative writing or fiction to read, but no present-day events, please. She came away telling me I had to read a newspaper every day, and I think that lasted about a week. She, though, seemed to be well-informed and highly impassioned in her day. Go, Mom! I am impressed with her political awareness and passion. I have never seen these before.

She has not yet received the magazines that Claudia has sent, but promises to *"place them in my waiting room, so patients may see them"* when they do arrive. She also seems disappointed that she has not yet met Joe Shine, although she is optimistic and thinks she may someday, since he doesn't live very far away from her. What a coincidence—how small and close their worlds are.

Wool to make a sweater is scarce in both countries, but Mom promises that if she finds some she will send it. I love how they exchange real things that are part of both of their worlds.

She closes her letter with a wish. *"I would, very much, like to come to France someday, but it is not easy. It requires much money. Perhaps if I am ever rich, I shall come. I should indeed love to.*

"Goodnight, dearest Raymonde. Write soon. Love, Sylvia. Paul sends his love too!"

This is now truly a family affair!

Sylvia holding Judy

Feathering the Nest

February 21, 1946

I get a slight shiver as I realize we are just a little over a year from my appearance on the scene, and I can hardly wait for the descriptions I am sure are coming of Mom's pregnancy, her (hopefully) happy feelings about it, and much more. I can't resist peeking ahead; the last letter is dated March 26, 1947—less than three months before my birth!

Judging by the level of detail about what my mother ate for breakfast and what boys she liked, I am sure I will learn things about my impending birth that I never knew before. I am very excited about every single detail! I can hardly wait, but I have committed to going through the letters one by one and then writing about each one as I come to it.

So, in February 1946, the year before my birth, Mom mentions a magazine about children that Claudia has sent her. Aha! The news must be out that she is considering having a baby, but where was it? Did I miss it? I think I have each letter in sequence. But maybe it was just a happy coincidence that Claudia sent magazines on this subject. Mom says she keeps the magazines in the waiting room of the office, *"so that all our patients may read them. They are very interesting, and everybody asks me where I get them. I am very proud to say to them that my friend from France sends them to me. I, too enjoy reading them very much,"* she adds, *"although I must confess that I do not have very much time to read."*

Mom, it appears, is keeping very, very busy in her new apartment, with her new husband and her new life—and apparently loving every minute of it! *"I love my new apartment very much, and Paul and I are very happy here. At first, I worried about how I would ever keep the house clean, but now I do a little each day and manage, too, to cook, shop and be the nurse for our patients."* I think about how immaculate she always kept our house while she held her treasured job as elementary school teacher for thirty-four years and raised my brother and me. She was starting on the path of supermom, it seems, right from the beginning of her marriage. I feel a sense of pride as I read more of the loving details. *"It is all very interesting, and the best part of it all is the fact that I have my Paul with me each day— all day long. It is truly wonderful!"* Once again, I feel the wonder of being able to be a fly on the wall of the relationship my parents had at the very beginning of their sixty-four-year marriage. "'Til death do us part" was the promise, and they kept that commitment, even with the ups and downs of their relationship that I witnessed.

Dad's practice has started growing. *"Slowly, we are building up a good practice, with nice patients. Some of them live in our (apartment) house, some are relatives and friends, and some come because they know the brother of Paul, whose name is Sam. He is a physician, and well-liked by his patients, so they are willing to come to Paul to have their teeth fixed."*

My Uncle Sam was always a kind of legend as I was growing up, and later Dad opened a new office in the same apartment as Sam's, on 167th Street and the Grand Concourse in the Bronx. There, they enjoyed many good years together as "the doctor and the dentist." They certainly made their parents proud! And Uncle Sam always made house calls to our family, as well as to many others. In fact, I learned that as a general practitioner he had delivered over five thousand babies, my brother and me among them. Coincidentally, he also delivered my daughter's pediatrician! Those days were so different from today's era of medical specialization!

Mom shares her sadness that Joe Shine, the American soldier who had taken an interest in Claudia while stationed in France, is on his way back to America. She worries about her friend, but also keeps her own matchmaking skills on the alert. *"I suppose you will miss him, though I hope you won't be <u>too</u> unhappy about his leaving. Perhaps you will meet another nice American boy. I wonder if Joe will come to see us when he gets home? I would be happy if he would, so he can tell us more about you, and about France. I shall let you know, of course, if he comes."*

The weather is a topic of conversation, but not just to fill the page. Sylvia describes a huge snowstorm that I remember reading about—an enormous one the winter before I was born, in which cars were buried. *"The wind howled, and the snow kept coming. "This morning, the snow was piled high, and everyone went to work shoveling the snow. We, of course, do not have to worry about cleaning the sidewalks, because the superintendent takes care of it."* I can feel her relief and pride at not having to address this huge task. *"In my mother's house (a small private house), we always had to worry about cleaning the snow away ourselves. It is great to live in a big apartment house. There are so many conveniences."* As I picture that big building, a humorous memory floats in. When we played outside, as we could do when we were six or seven, and we wanted to invite some other child to join us, we would yell at the top of our lungs, "Johnny's mother, can Johnny come out and play?" I haven't heard or thought about those words for close to sixty years but can hear them as if I had just shouted them. And if Johnny's mother did not respond, we kept on yelling until she opened the window, and usually said yes! It's fun to regain these snapshots from my past as my mother relates what is going on in her present to Claudia.

She has very little time for recreation, since they are always working. *"The only day we have some free time is on Sunday afternoon. At that time, we visit my mother and dad at their home, after which we usually go to see Paul's mother and dad."* No wonder my mother was so eager to have a regular, committed day or night for our growing family to visit my father and mother. Friday nights always belonged to my parents. They made this clear to us. This was even more of a requirement once our long-awaited daughter was born and then, since we had started so late, we adopted our son. No excuse for absence from Friday night dinner was a good one, as far as Mom was concerned, and this habit that she and my father had with their parents gives me a better insight into and understanding of the practice they wanted to see passed on.

"By that time, it is late, and we go home to bed. Sometimes, if we do not work late, we go to the movies on a Saturday night. Last week, we saw 'Confidential Agent' with Charles Boyer and Lauren Bacall. I like Charles Boyer very much. Do you like him, too?" My guess is that Claudia did—they enjoyed so many of the same movies and stars, and again I wish I could find a stash of letters that Sylvia saved, the way Claudia saved my mother's precious letters. I think again of all the writings of both of my parents that I had the good fortune to inherit, and how few of them I have read or catalogued. Maybe in one of these treasure troves I will find a packet of letters from Claudia. I know I will keep searching until I have gone through everything. What a pleasure it would be to find those!

She signs off in her reportorial style, *"I guess I will end my letter now, for there is a patient in the chair, and Paul will soon need me."* I love the view of her moment-to-moment existence in those new and exciting times. She of course inquires after Claudia's mother and reaffirms her wish to hear from her pen friend. *"I love to receive letters from you. They are very interesting."*

Somehow, she never seems to take their relationship for granted. And she seems to trust that it will continue, as it did, for just about forever. She needs to remind Claudia of her own caring and her desire to hear more from her pen pal. I guess she did a good job, as did her friend, since they continued until my mother began her serious decline. I know they would still be writing today if my mom had been able to maintain her love of language and communicating with her dear friend in a foreign land.

I feel a sadness and re-experience the loss and the unfairness of the way in which my mother's life ended. But I am soothed by knowing I have the spunky, energetic, busy, excited young woman—who was to become my incredible mother—to continue to get to know through these letters.

Judy + Sylvia celebrating at a cousin's bridal shower

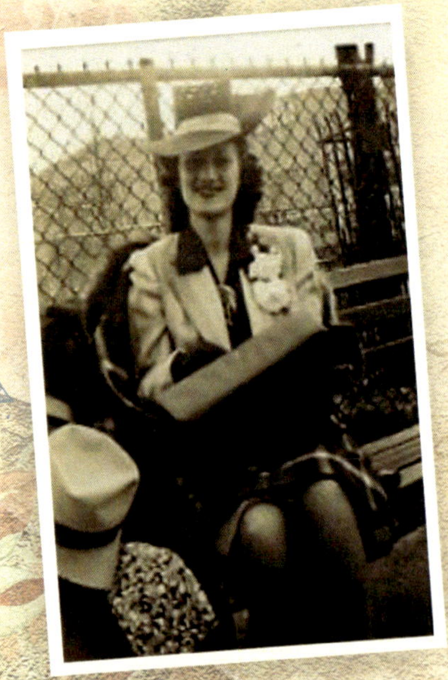

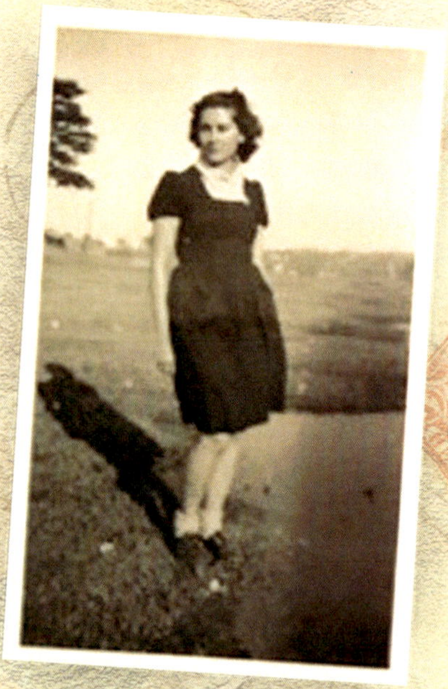

Soulmates and Strangers, bien sûr ...

June 3, 1946

Almost a year to the day before my birth! I can't wait to see how things led up to my dramatic (at least for me) entrance!

I am a little disappointed to see that this letter is written totally in English—as was the previous one, now that I think about it. I sense that Mom is so overwhelmed by all her obligations and duties running a dental practice and a household, maintaining a loving marriage and *beginning to think about having a baby* (I am hoping and assuming) that she simply doesn't have the mental bandwidth to make the attempt. She starts by apologizing for not having written to Claudia for a very long time (it appears to have been about four months since the last letter). *"Days slip by so quickly, I never have time for the things I must do. Tonight, however, while Paul is working on his patients, I shall start to write this letter to you, and hope I will not be interrupted before I finish writing."*

Then, I am surprised to discover, even with the end of the war over a year behind them, Sylvia speaks about all the suffering going on in Europe. *"We in America, do not suffer, but there is much trouble in politics, and there are many shortages—of food and clothing. These days, we have stopped eating bread, for the bread we don't eat goes to the starving people in Europe, we hope."* I shake my head in wonder as I read these words.

I remembered the expression that all of us kids ridiculed our parents for saying: "You have to finish everything on your plate, because there are starving children in Africa," they would say. Could that "silliness" (we couldn't see how our cleaning our plates would make children in Africa have more to eat), have started with the habit of not eating bread so that the children in Europe would have some, or was it more of a symbolic showing of sympathy? I feel a twinge of guilt for how I took part in the ridicule and mimicking. *"It is very difficult to buy meat,"* she continues. *"This week, the butcher is open only two days, for he says he has no meat to sell. Food is very expensive here, as well as in France."* No wonder there was always a preciousness assigned to our food—a hatred of waste, a need to "clean our plates" that I had never fully understood or appreciated before.

Then, once again Mom surprises me. *"As for politics,"* she muses, *"there have been, and still are, so many strikes, it is no wonder that industry cannot function normally. However, I suppose that is how it must be after a war, so we'll just hope it will all straighten out in the near future."* I just never saw—or remember seeing—such a politically aware, philosophical student of the world when I was growing up. I don't even remember her discussing upcoming elections with my father when I was old enough to know what was happening in the world, even if I didn't take an active interest in them (shame on me!) *"I know that your country is having its problems, as well,"* she continues. *"We read in the papers about your elections. Today's newspapers say that the Communists and Socialists are being defeated, and that the People's Party is coming into power. Is that so? I hope that whatever party is elected, it will mean better days for 'la belle France.'"*

I love the next part of the letter, in which she lets Claudia know how positively the returning American soldiers speak about her friend's country. *"Even though they are happy to be home, they are happy, too, that they*

saw your country. They speak very well of France."

She ends this letter by telling her friend how excited she is about being able to go away for two weeks to the mountains in July or August. She wonders if Claudia will be going to the seashore this summer. And I am wondering if Claudia has yet met the delightful Italian-born Frenchman she will marry, whom I will grow to love like a second father. I am surprised I have heard nothing of him, nor of anything about it being about time for Mom and Dad to start a family. As I calculate it, just when they return from their two weeks away that summer, I will be about to become more than a glint in my parents' eye, more than just a good idea, but an actual reality.

Why it is such a big deal to read about my beginnings through the eyes of my young mom-to-be? It is just a perspective I have never had, I think. I feel I will learn more about her process of choosing to have a child, a choice that was such a difficult one for me and resulted in a sixteen-year wait once my husband and I married.

But for now, there is no mention, and as she has been doing lately, she ends the letter with a delightful excuse: *"I will end now, for I must help Paul. He is very busy and needs my assistance. Write soon, Ray dear,"* she concludes.

August 8, 1946

In the next letter, Mom writes in French, for the first time in a long time. She takes note of that, as I do. *"I find it difficult. I love the French language very much, but I wish I could speak it well."* (Gee, it sure looks like she is writing it extremely well.) *"I studied it five years ago, and I have forgotten a lot,"* she writes sadly. I think of how each time I call Claudia, now ninety-one, she giggles at my attempts and says dramatically, in French of course, *"Oh, you have forgotten so much!!!"* And yet practically each time I break into French with a colleague or a stranger I hear speaking *la belle langue* on the street, I somehow manage to string whole bunches of words, phrases and even sentences together. These native French people almost always tell me how well I speak, but I know that Claudia has set a high standard for me, and that served me so well the summer I stayed with them in France.

Still, I deeply empathize with my mom, who is trying hard to get the words out. Just about the whole first page of this letter is in French, and she does amazingly well, I think. I never knew she had such facility with it. We could have spoken to one another and practiced together once I returned from France that summer. *"Writing the French language is harder than speaking it, isn't it?"* she asks. Then she breaks into English and reveals, *"Yes, I do still converse in French with my demobilized friend. It is always great sport when we speak French*

together. He speaks French very rapidly, and I must always tell him to speak slower, before I can understand him. He loves the French language very much and is going to college now to study to be an interpreter. He has a very good wife, for she works, while he goes to college. He must go for another year, and then he will be ready to look for a job. He may even go to work in Lyon someday," she says, always trying to connect, connect, connect. *"Who knows? He likes France, and would like to live there someday."*

Now my mother surprises me yet again. Claudia apparently asked her if she has ever been to a boxing match. *"No, I have never been to one. I, like you, listen to them over the radio,"* she says. Apparently her interest in the sport has not yet faded. Will wonders never cease? *"I have no desire to see one,"* she continues. *"There is too much bloodshed and it is not pretty to see two men fight each other. I enjoy listening to the fight over the radio, however, when Joe Louis fights."* This is amazing, given her total insistence on nonviolence as my brother and I were growing up.

Then comes another revelation: *"Once or twice a year, we go to see a baseball game at the Yankee Stadium. I enjoy that very much."* Really, Mom? I never knew that you liked baseball. Once in a while in my childhood we all went to a Yankee game as a family, but it was rare, and I thought she more tolerated than enjoyed it! *"Do you play baseball in France? I don't think you do,"* she continues. And I think she was right. *"In America, everyone loves*

baseball. *Even the 5-year old youngsters are able to tell you the names of the baseball teams, and the names of the men on each team. I have a 13-year old nephew who would rather listen to the ballgame over the radio than go swimming in the lake where he is spending his summer."* I never realized that the baseball passion was so great in her day. While it still is in ours, there is so much else to choose from that we do not have the all-encompassing obsession with the game that she describes.

She concludes her (usual) four-page letter by recounting the week she and my father spent in Connecticut at his "physician brother's" home. About how enjoyable it was to swim in the lake, row, fish, walk, eat and more. I remember that lake and the times we went there as a family later on. It was pleasant and fun when the brothers were getting along—which was not always the case. She wishes Claudia a wonderful vacation too: *"Vacation time is so short—working time is so long. It does not seem fair,"* she complains. And then her traditional sign off: *"Paul and I send our best love to you and your mother."*

I keep wondering when Claudia will meet and marry Mario—I think it should be about time, but I guess I will have to wait for the few remaining letters to hopefully mention these important events (and my impending arrival). I now wish I had all the letters that went back and forth for the seventy years they were *correspondantes*, but also recognize how full of appreciation I am to have at least the gift of these early communications! They have

1948

Mario and Claudia meet at last

given me the greatest access to the young girl who grew to be the young woman who became my mother. I am once again deeply grateful, especially now that I can't reach out to her directly and discuss these things with her. She would have loved that kind of conversation before her serious illness took over. She would have been so flattered—and probably surprised—by my interest.

But if I am to be honest, I was so focused on my own life and its challenges and joys that I question whether I would have taken the time and felt the interest to explore the letters with her, even when I could. I feel guilty about that, knowing the probable answer. But I think I can replace the guilt with gratitude at having them now, and feeling my mother's energy, youth, and delightful presence. Perhaps she is aware of this enthusiasm from some higher plane of existence. I hope so. I am, after all, my mother's daughter, and I am proud of who she was and who she became. And I know how proud she would be of me, especially after I celebrated the launch of my first book, *The Power of Acknowledgment* with two others that followed. Reading and sharing these letters is a way to deeply *acknowledge* both my mother and her cherished pen pal, my French mother. So it's very fitting, if not completely satisfying.

But I once again mourn the unfair way her deeply caring, loving life came to an end. I must learn to accept this, but am not yet able to do that. Maybe focusing on the brightness of her younger years will help me find my peace.

Sylvia and Paul's Legacy.

Carl, Judy, Paul, & Sylvia

Bob, Judy, Stefanie & Jared

Sylvia with Judy
"Under Construction"

A New Year, A New Life?

January 15, 1947

We are at last in the year of my birth! I am getting pretty excited about this, and will certainly look for clues about my impending arrival in these last few letters. Mom, you are three months pregnant—do you even know it yet? That is an amazing thought for me—I might know it now in this visit to the past—before she knows it! How strange and fascinating!

She starts off the letter in French, saying that she wanted to write for a whole month, but that she was always too busy. Then she breaks into English: *"I think I had better continue in English. It seems that I am forgetting more and more French,"* which is so sad for me to read, as I have gone and continue to go through this, too. *"I very rarely speak French, and my college days, when I learned how to speak and write French, seem very far away. It is five years, now, since I was graduated from college. So much has happened since then."*

And yes, so much *has* happened—a world war, a marriage, the establishment of my father's dental practice, the finding and creation of a home and an office, the beginning of a life ...

"Perhaps, some day when my children study French in their schools, I shall learn and remember it once more," she muses and I get a twinge of guilt again. We never spoke the language we both loved so dearly, except when Mario and Claudia finally came to America. And then we all stumbled in both languages. *"It is sad how much we forget of what we learn!"* The amazing discovery, though, Mom, is that when we are back in the environment in which French is spoken, words that have been locked away resurface. Every time I go to visit Mario and Claudia, or visit a French-speaking country like Morocco, I am shocked at how much I remember—how words come zooming into my consciousness that I didn't even remember that I knew. This is encouraging to me as I struggle with my phone conversations with Mario and Claudia, for if I were back in France I know I would remember more and I would do better. I would have liked to reassure you, Mom, about that as well.

Then Sylvia speaks of the recently passed holiday season. *"In our country,"* she says, *"the Christmas week is the nicest time of year. Store windows are gay, as are the people who shop in the stores. Everyone seems to forget his troubles during that week."* I am a little surprised to hear her say this, as the household of her younger years was devoutly Jewish, and it was considered slightly "sinful" to celebrate or, I would guess, even appreciate Christian holidays. Maybe she wrote that in deference to Claudia's background. She speaks then of a gathering of all her sisters and their families, her brother and his girlfriend and her parents at their home—the first time they were all there together. She talks of an exchange of gifts, of eating and sitting around and chatting. Next week, she will be inviting all of Dad's family for a similar kind of celebration. I am guessing that this was their Chanukah celebration, but there is no mention of the name of the holiday. Interesting ... and a bit strange. Why would she not mention that? Was she concerned about some prejudice that Claudia might feel toward her for her Jewish heritage based on what had occurred during the Nazi era in France?

Later she would warn me about prejudice against Jews, whenever I would go on one of my French voyages. But it was so far from my consciousness when I was there, usually surrounded by the warmth of Mario and Claudia and their friends and family, that I always pooh-poohed it.

Now she is sharing the American way of celebrating

New Year's Eve. *"We spent a very pleasant New Year's Eve, at a friend's house. She had a party, and we all had lots of fun. There was plenty of noise at midnight. Everyone blew horns and shouted, 'Happy New Year.' Over the radio, we listened to what went on at Broadway. Everyone went wild. Boys tried to climb telephone poles. Everyone kissed everybody else. Many people were drunk. Is there so much excitement in France on New Year's Eve?"* I think back to the old films of my parents that I recently had transferred to DVDs. How shocked I was at one of the New Year's Eve celebrations that showed my mother and father dancing very slowly and romantically, and then—shock of shocks, horror of horrors—I saw my puritanical mother (at least on that subject) *smoking*! And, it appeared, *inhaling*! In that home movie, Mom was looking stunning, sexy, and a little wild, I might add. Maybe it was the same party that she was describing to Claudia. I don't know if the films are dated, but now I have a desire to check to see if they match up.

Next she gives her opinion of a child named Roselyne who must have stayed with Claudia for a while. *"I think, perhaps, her parents might have spoiled her.... She will change, I am sure, when she is older."*

I wonder if this Roselyne had anything to do with Mario and Claudia deciding not to have children. One time when Claudia and I were telling each other of the important role each of us had played in the other's life, she said that they never needed to have children, as they had me as a daughter! I smiled and still glow over that comment, even if I knew in my heart that it was only a part of the truth.

Mom once more asks about the American boys in France, most of whom, she surmises, must have returned home. *"I think you have learned a lot more English, since knowing American boys,"* she assumes. *"Are they very different from French boys?"* I wish I could have read Claudia's response to that question!

Claudia, Judy & her daughter, Stefanie

Then she tells Claudia how happy she was that Claudia liked *Coronet*. Apparently, this was the *Reader's Digest* of the day. Mom wants to know if Claudia was able to read and understand everything. *"I think they have very nice pictures, as well as interesting articles, don't you? I hope you enjoy it."*

She closes, because she must go make dinner, with, *"Please write as soon as you can. Love, and a HAPPY NEW YEAR from Paul and Sylvia."* She has started including my dad in all these letters, which I find touching.

Wednesday, March 26 47

Ma chère Raymonde

    Tout est calme aujourd'hui, comme j'écris cette lettre. Dedans, il n'y a pas de bruit, à l'exception du sifflement du radiateur (do you have steam heat in your apartment?) Dehors, il se fait de neige, mais il n'y a pas du vent. C'est le printemps, enfin! Je l'attends! À bientôt, il se fera beau et chaud... *le printemps*'
Je l'...

Mlle. Raymonde Bouillard
20 rue Cavenne
Lyon (7e)
France

The Last Letter

March 26, 1947

This is the last of the letters I have from my mother as a young woman, written to and preserved, for all these years, by Claudia. I am palpitating a bit, feeling a bit weepy, knowing I will shortly be saying goodbye to the young woman I have just come to know so newly and so well. I don't want to read this last letter. I want to treasure the upcoming connection forever, and still know that there will always be a place for me to come to discover my mother in her newness and her journey. I know that my birth is right around the corner—a mere two and a half months away. I must clearly be feeling my mother's emotions, her tiredness, her suspense as she writes, waiting for my arrival. What will she say about this amazing process she is undergoing? What details of this miracle will she share with her transatlantic best friend?

Oh, she is writing in French—a whole paragraph rather than just a sentence this time! *"Everything is calm today, so I am writing this letter. Inside, there is no noise, with the exception of the hiss of the radiator."* Wow, her vocabulary is excellent! She inserts a phrase in English, in parentheses: *"Do you have steam heat in your apartment?"* Then back to French: *"Outside, there are clouds, but no wind. It is finally the Spring. I am waiting for it! Soon it will be beautiful and hot. Do you like the Spring? It is my favorite of all of the seasons."* Any news about being less than three months away from giving birth? This is more like a weather report, Mom! *"I am not going outdoors today"* (we are back to English now), *"for I have a cold, so I thought it would be a good opportunity to write to you today. Every one of our friends has a cold these days. The weather is so changeable. Last Friday was a lovely spring day (March 21st). This week, however, we have had winter blizzards and snow. Is it like that in France? I guess winter is having her last fling, before she goes away for another year."*

Next, she wishes Claudia a very happy birthday, now that she is twenty-seven, and states that she, Sylvia, will be twenty-six in September. That means she was ten years younger than I was when I had my first child—quite a difference. I had waited so long because I was nervous about motherhood affecting my career and my health (due to my type 1 diabetes). Then she compliments Claudia on her great memory: *"You were right, too, about my wedding anniversary. You have a remarkable memory. We were married three years this February. My husband was very kind to me. As gifts, he sent me a bottle of perfume, a corsage of an orchid (which I adore! They are so expensive, I've only received 3 or 4 of them in my lifetime) and he gave me a present of some money, as well. I thought he was exceedingly generous."* This is impressive; I can only ever remember Dad giving Mom a card with $25 in it—forever! What a sweet celebration this special one back in time must have been.

Claudia & Mario

For her part: *"I bought him a shirt and tie, and a rack to put his pipes away on. He smokes a pipe and has several of them around the house."* Dad smoked a pipe? That's news to me! I can kind of imagine him with one, and in my mind's eye, he looks pretty classy and cool.

Now it's on to a description of a wedding of a friend, apparently after Claudia has told her about a wedding she attended. So, when is Claudia getting married to that sweet, dear man, Mario, of whom I am so fond? Sylvia hasn't mentioned him yet. Maybe he comes later?

The wedding Mom attended was in a large banquet hall. There were about seventy-five couples there. *"After the wedding ceremony, we had a delicious turkey dinner. [The bride's] parents paid $30 for each couple, for the dinner, which is a lot of money. After dinner, there were cigars and liquor, and dancing to an orchestra. It was very nice. She and her new husband have gone to Bermuda for their honeymoon."* All of this seems to have a touch of envy in it—I don't think my parents had any honeymoon when they married, just one night at the Plaza Hotel in New York City, but I can't be sure. It makes me sad that there is no one I can turn to who will know this now.

She adds, *"I think they will be very happy, for they are deeply in love with each other. He was in the army for 3 years—in the Pacific and served in Japan for about a year."* Mom, there is only one page left of this last letter. *Where am I?* You are six months pregnant, so now you must know about me! Why aren't you filling all four pages with details about the miracle—of me? I am afraid to turn to the last page. This is it ...

And then I laugh out loud. At the top of the last page of the last letter I see this: *"I may think seriously about having a child in a few months. We shall see!"* Mom, you

Bob & Judy Wedding

won't be thinking about it—you will be holding that child in your arms in a few months! What gives here? The only explanation I can imagine is that my mother didn't want to make her friend jealous, not only of her husband, but of her impending motherhood. I guess I will never figure this one out, and have no one to ask now.

Judy & Bob today

Then she makes another mysterious comment: *"As for a name, I haven't thought too much about it. Paul likes the name of Robert for a boy."* Isn't that ironic? That is my husband's name. *"I like it, too,"* she continues. *"I like Barbara, for a girl. Do you?"* Now wait just a minute! My cousin Barbara will be born three weeks later, on April 14th. Did the two sisters fight over who got the name for her daughter if it was a girl, and did her big sister, Esther, win? Or was it that they both thought of the name and didn't share their choice with one another? That is another question I will probably never know the answer to.

And that's it for me, for motherhood, for the name

"Judy" my parents ultimately agreed upon, for the total change in Sylvia's life. Not another mention. We go on to plans for a wonderful sounding summer vacation that Claudia and her husband will be taking. Mom admires these exciting plans, because *"We hear so much about the Riviera, here in America, that I should like to go there someday, too. Is it as wonderful as they say it is? It must be lovely there at Easter."* Then she says something else that mystifies me: *"We will not go anyplace this Easter,"* which is, I surmise, at least in part because Easter doesn't exist for this Jewish family. What happened to Passover? Again, I wonder if Mom was concerned that Claudia would have some judgment against her if she spoke of her Judaism.

"Paul's father is going away for a week, so we must stay with his mother, who is an invalid. They have a maid to care for her, but the maid goes out Wednesday and Saturday night, so we will have to sleep there those nights." I remember the stories of how devoted my father was to his very ill mother. Mom doesn't seem resentful—it is just a fact that this must be done. I don't remember my father's mother, who died when I was only two, while I do have many incredibly happy and loving memories of my mother's mother, who passed away when I was eight.

And now, the end of the last letter that I have in my possession: *"Happy Easter to you and your mother. Write to me when you can. I love to hear from you. Paul asks to be remembered, too. Love, Sylvia."*

I weep as I read the last letter from my mother that I will ever see. But I have a new set of memories now, thanks to Claudia—priceless memories of the mother I always loved so dearly but never knew as a young girl and as a young woman.

I am truly grateful to Claudia for saving these treasures and leaving them as her legacy to me. There is no greater inheritance she and my mother could have left me. Few women can say they knew their mother as a young girl, from before their own birth, as I have come to know mine. And for that gift I am, and will forever be, truly blessed and thankful.

♥

Fin

About the Author, Judith Umlas

Judith's first experience with writing in order to make a difference was her article "How Not to Talk to a Pregnant Businesswoman," published by *Working Woman* in 1986. It became the cover story and landed Judith a guest appearance on *Good Morning America*, where she discovered that she was considered to be the "expert" on this demoralizing situation which had bothered so many women in the past. Afterward came the book she authored for IIL Publishing, *The Power of Acknowledgment,* which launched her career in corporate training at the International Institute for Learning (IIL) in 2006. *Grateful Leadership: Using the Power of Acknowledgment to Engage All Your People and Achieve Superior Results* in 2013 made Judith a keynote attraction for conferences around the world. And lastly came *You're Totally Awesome! The Power of Acknowledgment for Kids*. (All of these books can be found on the **gratefulleadership.com** website.)

This latest book, *Soulmates & Strangers*, is a very personal memoir honoring the mother who gave birth to her, Sylvia Handler Wagreich, and the French mother, Claudia Raymonde Bouillard Mariotti, who birthed Judith's love for, and competency in, the French language, which she adored then and still does today.

Judy's parents with her daughter Stefanie

Acknowledgments

First and foremost, I acknowledge both the mother who gave birth to me, Sylvia Handler Wagreich, who loved me "to all four corners of her heart," as she used to say, and her French pen pal, or *correspondante*, Claudia Mariotti, my "French mother." Their passion, connection, persistence, and love of each other's languages and cultures benefited both of them tremendously, and especially me, as the grateful beneficiary of their unique relationship.

I must also acknowledge my French father, Mario, who helped create the most incredible summer for me when he said "Yes!" to Claudia's request that was initiated by my mother that I stay with the couple in France. I'm grateful that he and I were able to keep in regular, meaningful touch, even after Claudia passed away. His wonderful aide, Christelle Ance, arranged bi-weekly Skype meetings for us until the end of his life at age 96 in May, 2021. And I also found that he really meant it when he said he only knew about three words in English, so I would have to speak French exclusively when I came to stay with them for the summer between high school and college! Claudia said the same (though I later found out that she knew a lot more than she let on) so that I would have little choice but to speak the language I had become so passionate about. So by the time I left at the end of that summer, I was dreaming in French and speaking close to fluently!

Then there are the dear friends of Mario and Claudia, Alain and Claudine Bouvier, whom I had the pleasure of meeting when I spent that wonderful summer in France, and later on their wonderful children Fabrice and Florence who came to visit my family in New York. Alain, Claudine, and especially Fabrice have played a vital role in helping me stay connected to this day to Mario until the end of his life, after my dearest Claudia passed away some years back. Fabrice has tolerated my French, much less fluent now than what I spoke that summer, and has helped me maintain my vital connection to Mario and thus to my French mother, Claudia—and therefore to my own mother as well.

I also acknowledge my dear son, Jared, who wanted to visit Mario and Claudia, taste French foods, and hear the "ear tickling" language I spoke about to him when

I gave him the choice of going on a trip anywhere as a special gift to him. What he really wanted was a taste of that wonderful summer I had had with them and spoke about so often, to see where I had stayed and more. This led to our wonderful trip to France when he was fourteen, to some delightful times with my French parents, and to the priceless gift Claudia gave me when she presented me with my mother's letters to her that she had preserved.

My dear friend, Dr. Chrys Ghiraldini, also played a vital role in another of the trips I took when I was very concerned about Mario and Claudia as they faced some of the severe challenges of aging. She wouldn't give up her (not so) gentle persistence in urging me to make the trip, or I would regret it forever. So off I went, and had an amazingly intimate and meaningful time connecting with Mario and Claudia once again. It was on that trip that I finally summoned the courage to read the letters my young and spirited mother had written to Claudia—giving me insights into her life and opinions and pop culture expertise that no other daughter I knew had ever had the good fortune to have.

Another dear friend who played a vital role, especially with the creation of this book, is Renee Avery-Boyd, Principal in Avery Design Solutions. Renee is a fellow seeker and spiritual soul sister with whom I connected deeply almost as soon as we met. She "adopted" this passion project of mine as though it was one of her beloved rescue animals and helped me bring it to a state of vitality, potential impact and beauty that I could not have envisioned without her incredible input, nurturance and creativity. She created the covers of the book in such a way that I felt they were "channeled" by my mother to her, even using my mother's favorite color without my saying a word about this to her, the peach color you see. I'll always be grateful to her for her true love of both me and my passion project.

And Maria Scharf, Owner/Principal of Maria Scharf Design is a colleague with whom I've worked on various books for IIL Publishing. Therefore she was someone I went to right away to design the very special interior of this book, filled with letters from my mother to her dear pen pal, recipes, poems and much more that are so vital to the telling and emotional impact of this story. She and I have put in what seem to be endless hours on the design and continuous redesign given the perfectionistic tendencies we both share, until we have created it to be so exactly right that I cry every time I review the absolutely gorgeous design. I think Maria would agree that this book represents the most work she ever invested into any book project, even someone else's "passion project." So I know it has been a major investment of time, energy, creativity, despair, rework and much more. All have led to a book of which I couldn't be prouder.

Melina Africa, Operations Manager of IIL Printing is someone who has gone so "above and beyond" in printing various formats, papers, covers and more of this book that I feel she desesrves special appreciation and acknowledgment. She also read the book from cover to cover early on, and was one of the first people to read it who was not associated with the storyline in some way. She read the book at a very challenging time in her life and said it provided a very wonderful and timely distraction. I'm grateful to her for going through so many interations of the book that have helped bring it to the beautiful state in which you find it today.

Then there's Mary Tiegreen, master photographer and designer in Palisades, NY where I live, who was recommended to me to give her input to the design process at a challenging point. Her sample design of a section of my book gave the creative process a whole new flavor and feel, so I'm also grateful to her for communicating her vision clearly to our team which then put its own "stamp" on it (literally and figuratively).

Of course, I must acknowledge my husband, Bob Umlas, who supports everything I do! He fell in love with Mario and Claudia after I returned from that first trip when I told him that they said I should marry him, even though I was still in my teens when he first proposed! They liked everything I told them about him. We had many special times with them as we got the chance to show them our country, which was as meaningful to us as their opportunities to show me France and other parts of Europe had been for them!

My daughter Stefanie Armstrong and her precious

family, her husband, Shaun, and their two amazing children, Lilith and Lucius, are always on my acknowledgment list. Stefanie has inspired me with her gift of writing and of creating a truly inspiring and soon to be published memoir. Another person always on my list is my mother's mother, Lena Handler. My precious grandmother always told me and demonstrated to me what a special person I was. As a result, I think I have come to believe her and am finally living into her vision, making it mine.

And I acknowledge my father, Paul Wagreich, DDS, who seemed to love the beautiful relationship of Sylvia and Claudia. He even wrote in French to Claudia when he first married my mother, and supported her passion for her friend and her friend's culture for all the years he witnessed them.

I acknowledge my brother Dr. Carl Wagreich, who had a similar experience to mine, also with our parents' blessing, but living with a family in Mexico. This experience later influenced his decision to co-direct "The Baja Project for Crippled

Children," now called Operation Footprint. The Project consists of podiatrists who treat as well as perform surgery at no cost to disabled Mexican children. While there he met his wonderful wife, Edna, a translator from that country. Now all four of their sons speak fluent Spanish.

And I'm grateful to E. LaVerne Johnson, the Founder, President & CEO of International Institute for Learning, Inc. for her continuous support of my discovering and expressing my true voice, through the books I write. I know this latest book is due at least in part to her influence and confidence in me.

Finally, I acknowledge all who value the experience of sharing families, languages, and cultures in such meaningful ways as my brother and I did. To all of the student exchange programs that exist to facilitate this—you're doing important and never-to-be-forgotten work for so many lucky students. These young people get to live with families of different cultures and traditions, and to remember and be influenced by that experience and by the families forever, as I was by mine.

"Cast of Characters"

Sylvia Handler Wagreich, Claudia's pen pal, *Judy's mother*
- **Lena and Mannie Handler**, Sylvia's mother & father, *Judy's maternal grandparents*

Paul Wagreich, husband of Sylvia, *Judy's father*
- **Celia and Frank Wagreich**, Paul's mother & father, *Judy's paternal grandparents*

Judy Wagreich Umlas, Sylvia's daughter & the author
Bob Umlas, *husband of Judy*
- **Stefanie Armstrong & Jared Umlas**, *Judy's children*
  - **Lilith & Lucius Armstrong**, Stefanie's children
  - **Shaun Armstrong**, Stefanie's husband

- **Esther Handler Serber**, Sylvia's oldest sister
  - **Joan Serber**, Esther's older daughter
  - **Barbara Serber Leff**, Esther's younger daughter
- **Adeline Handler Cohen**, Sylvia's 2nd oldest sister
  - **Joyce Cohen Goldenberg**, Adeline's daughter

"La Galerie des Personnages"

Claudia Raymonde Bouillard Mariotti, Sylvia's Pen pal
    Jeanne Seguin, Claudia's mother,
Mario Mariotti, husband of Claudia

Closest friends of Mario and Claudia:
Georgette Bouvier (nicknamed Zézette)
René Bouvier
    Alain Bouvier,
    son of Georgette & René
and
Madeleine Françon
Michel Françon
    Claudine Françon Bouvier,
    daughter of Madeleine & Michel
Alain and Claudine Bouvier, parents of:
    Fabrice Bouvier, son of Alain & Claudine,
    godson of Mario & Claudia
    Judy's main contact to Mario, husband of Claudia,
    in his later years until his death in 2021
    Florence Bouvier, daughter of Alain & Claudine